P9-DVB-864

15614

INFORMATION RESOURCES CENTER
ASIS INTERNATIONAL

SEP 0 4 2009

HV
6432.5
.O114
2009

Executive Protection:
Rising to the Challenge

by
Robert L. Oatman, CPP

ASIS
INTERNATIONAL
Advancing Security Worldwide®

Executive Protection:
Rising to the Challenge

Copyright © 2009 ASIS International

ISBN 978-1-887056-94-6

All rights reserved. No part of this publication may be reproduced, stored in a retrieval system, or transmitted, in any form or by any means, electronic, mechanical, photocopying, recording, or otherwise, without the prior written consent of the copyright owner.

The topics discussed in this book represent the opinions and personal judgments of the author and of professionals with whom he has consulted in the course of preparing this work. As each situation encountered by the protection professional will vary, so necessarily will the appropriate response. As the specific policies and procedures to be followed by individual professionals may vary according to the laws of each state, the conscientious professional should consult with his or her legal counsel before adopting guidelines and procedures.

Printed in the United States of America

10 9 8 7 6 5 4 3 2 1

First edition

Published by

ASIS International
1625 Prince Street
Alexandria, VA 22314-2818
703.519.6200

Oatman's book illustrates a keen understanding of private sector executive protection. His EP methods skillfully blend the proven elements of risk assessment, logistical planning, and close-in personal protection with an emphasis on the business world's need for low-key protection, cost-effectiveness, and methods that do not rely on special legal powers.

Edward J. Marinzel
Deputy Assistant Director for Protective Operations
United States Secret Service, Retired

Bob Oatman's expertise in executive protection helped guide us through the complexities of developing and managing an effective EP program. In his chapter "EP Needed As Never Before," Bob provides an insightful real-world view of executive risk in today's environment, reinforcing the rule that *hope is not a strategy* when it comes to protecting your executives.

Vance Toler, CPP
Director, Corporate Security
Southwest Airlines Co.

While tasked with protecting the U.S. Attorney General, members of my protective detail and I attended Oatman's seven-day EP training course. His approach to executive protection, in both the course and this book, strikes the right balance between security theory and real-world practice.

Vincent Fazzio
Supervisory Special Agent, FBI, Retired
U.S. Attorney General's Protection Detail

You will find a number of consultants and organizations offering training and support in the area of executive protection. For me, simply put, Bob Oatman is the best. My responsibility, like that of other security directors, includes safeguarding our corporate assets and executives. Bob's domestic and international scope, knowledge, personal practical experience, and business acumen have provided me with the necessary tools to effectively do my job. The book pulls this together in a clear, comprehensive manner, and I would recommend it as a must-read for security directors and others responsible for executive protection in their businesses. It is insightful and will prepare you well.

James Danylyshyn
Director, Corporate Security
Xerox Corporation

In today's dynamic executive protection environment, there is little substitute for exacting standards and applied experience. For more than 20 years, Robert Oatman has been a leading practitioner, teacher, and writer in executive protection. He has set the standard while protecting his clients and while educating the thousands of students and practitioners who have read his previous books or passed through his highly regarded executive protection training programs. Bob draws on the hard-won lessons from his career to provide us with practical, hands-on solutions to the challenges EP specialists face in the real world. I have benefited from training with Bob and commend his quiet, professional approach to the art of executive protection.

Gordon McIntosh
Special Agent in Charge, Protective Services Unit
The World Bank

Dedication

To the Executive Protection Professionals,
those dedicated men and women
who devote their time, energy, and expertise
in the protection of corporate executives,
government officials, and private families.

Acknowledgments

This book, like my other two books on executive protection, was developed from a personal timeline that has shaped my career both in law enforcement and in my own business for over 40 years. My success in this specialized security field is the result of decades of developing a network of professional colleagues, strengthened by the support of family and friends. I believe strongly that to succeed in any endeavor, you should recognize your strengths, identify your weaknesses, and, most important, surround yourself with honest, sincere people who generously share their positive energy.

This book would not have been possible without the input and support of family and professionals who have shared their knowledge and ideas. There are so many colleagues and friends to thank that I know I will miss some individuals, and for that I apologize in advance. My first acknowledgment is to my wife, Janice, and my two children, Rob (active duty Commander in the U.S. Coast Guard) and Andrea (office manager with our firm), who have given their time and attention to this project. I also wish to acknowledge Rick Heaps, who has spent 20 years managing our firm and being engaged in its day-to-day operations. I thank the expert faculty of our executive protection training programs, who have dedicated their time and expertise in training executive protection specialists from around the world and who continue to keep the training experience relevant and realistic.

To those who have lent their expertise and perspectives to

this book I owe a debt of gratitude: Bruce McIndoe and the iJET team for their insights into the world of intelligence; Gordon McIntosh for his hands-on experience in dealing with EP support on a global platform; and Bill Archer, who continues to share his years of experience. I thank Rudolph Giuliani for his insightful foreword to the book. To the security professionals who endorsed this work—Vance Toler, James Danylyshyn, Edward Marinzel, Vincent Fazzio, and Gordon McIntosh—I offer my thanks for their expertise and kind words of support.

Acknowledgment must also go to the executive protection specialists and directors of security who do this job every day, tackling the many challenges they meet along the way. I have been fortunate to gain not only their counsel but also their friendship. In particular, let me thank John Huvane, Giuliani Partners; Mike Bruggeman, CPP, General Motors; Mark Cheviron and Jeff Larner, Archer Daniels Midland; the FBI's Tim Williams, CPP, a friend who lends his expertise generously; Tony Silva, Harrah's Entertainment (who does this task most times by himself); Wayne Ross, CPP, Constellation Energy; the Aetna security team, headed by David Gionfriddo; and, finally, Nelson Abreu, a mentor and true EP professional.

I also thank my EP team: Tom Levering, CPP; Brian Feser, CPP; Dale Stonesifer; Bill Benedetto; and Keith Warner. They make EP, a particularly difficult job, look easy. Special thanks also go to the alumni of our seven-day executive protection training programs since 1996, who do this work 24/7 and on whom I rely for support and close-in protection wherever and whenever the need arises.

ASIS International's Evangeline Pappas, Ursula Uszynski, Susan Melnicove, and Vinn Truong have generously provided invaluable support in my publishing and teaching efforts.

I would also like to thank Peter Ohlhausen of Ohlhausen Research, Inc., who collaborates with me in conducting EP risk assessments for clients and who applied his excellent research and writing skills and wide security knowledge to help me develop this book.

Robert L. Oatman

President, R. L. Oatman & Associates, Inc.

July 2009

Foreword

When the bell rings, a boxer springs from his corner. Countless hours of exercise, training, and study have readied him for the task. Now, at the fateful moment, he is switched on and prepared to win. The bout may be long or short, lost or won, but one thing's certain: after all the preparation, the fight's outcome will be decided now.

Some jobs positively require high performance, deep preparation, and fast response. In my roles as a U.S. Attorney, Mayor of New York City, worldwide public speaker, and head of an international corporate consulting firm, I have seen the value of being prepared and having the confidence to take the right steps at key moments. When much is at stake, you have a great responsibility to be ready.

Security—executive protection in particular—is certainly one of those jobs. I know that from experience. As Mayor of New York, as I labored long and hard to help our city crush crime, some disturbing, irrational, but violent threats came my way. Now, in my speeches around the globe and in my consulting work for Giuliani Partners and legal work with Bracewell & Giuliani, I travel extensively and place myself before thousands of people. I expect my detail to be prepared—trained, practiced, informed, and ready to act.

The stakes are high in executive protection—often a matter of life and death for executives and the organizations they lead. At home and around the world, executives can be in harm's way. They are injured in car crashes, through medical emergencies, and in hotel fires. They may be targeted specifically, or their extensive travels and varied activities may boost their risk of being in the wrong place at the wrong time. As September 11, 2001, showed me and the rest of the world, a terrible attack can occur at any time, even on a beautiful, clear day when you least expect it.

Leaders can't lead and serve their organizations if they must worry (legitimately) about being attacked, harassed, injured, or unsafe. However, if able, knowledgeable, trusted security staff can free them from those worries, leaders can focus on their jobs and take full advantage of the opportunities they seek. An unprotected executive who travels to an unsafe destination or who stands alone before attackers can't do what his organization needs: lead. That executive will be preoccupied with his own security, or he may be harmed and hence unable to serve, perhaps ever again.

At Giuliani Partners, we provide professional guidance to leaders, based on six fundamental principles: integrity, optimism, courage, preparedness, communication, and accountability. These are the key principles I have learned through years of work in challenging posts, and they apply as well to the vital task of executive protection. An EP specialist needs integrity because he holds a trusted, inside position where he is privy to sensitive information. Optimism is required to persevere in the face of the job's challenges. An EP specialist needs courage to fight against dangerous adversaries, and preparedness is the best way to antic- ipate, avoid, or react to attacks. Communication (between the EP specialist and the protectee and between the EP program and other organizational departments) is essential for determin- ing what must be done and how to do it. Finally, EP specialists' accountability enables leaders to depend on them for this most important task.

In this, his third book on executive protection, Bob Oatman expands on his model for safeguarding leaders. That model, based on risk assessment, intelligence, risk avoidance, and constant planning for the "what if?" scenarios, has benefited me and my protective detail over the years. It's a sensible, rational, effective approach, one that empowers leaders to focus on leading, not on dodging attacks.

A final note: Some executives who would seem to need security services (because of the risks they face) feel reluctant to sign on to executive protection. They might think protection will be cumbersome, or they might fear how protection will be viewed by others.

These reluctant protectees shouldn't be afraid to use executive protection. The best leaders surround themselves with— and trustingly delegate certain responsibilities to—good people. They don't try to do everything themselves. Executives who face above-average levels of risk should therefore feel comfortable in delegating some of the responsibility for their security to well-chosen, highly skilled protection professionals.

Rudolph W. Giuliani
Mayor, New York City (1994-2001)
Chairman and Chief Executive Officer, Giuliani Partners LLC

Contents

1.
Leading Edge EP

Executive protection (EP)—the task of keeping key personnel safe from intentional and unintentional harm—is a widespread, recognized specialty in the security field. Its purpose is to safeguard people who face an above-average level of risk or whose security is especially important to an organization. This book focuses mainly on the protection of corporate executives but also addresses protective service for wealthy individuals (and, of course, those two categories often overlap), as well as low-key government details for federal judges or cabinet members. Typically, EP is performed by corporate employees for a corporation's top tier of executives, by family employees for all family members, by outside contractors, or by a combination of EP professionals.

Executive protection defends individuals from deliberate attacks and accidental harm (including car crashes, hotel fires, and medical emergencies)—but it also does much more. EP preserves valuable corporate assets (the principals), protects the corporate reputation (against deliberate embarrassment), protects corporate proprietary information (by minimizing the use of public transportation and otherwise being in the company of strangers, where data may be overheard or left behind), increases the security of other employees and family members, frees the principals from concern over their security, increases productivity (through facilitation of movements), and improves quality of life. Many corporations believe they have a duty to their shareholders to protect their top human assets and, by doing so, protect their brand.

Large corporations have operated EP programs for years, and the practice is expanding. Despite some corporations' recent concerns (during the 2008-2009 recession) that shareholders, the government, and the media might view executive protection as an excessive perk for protectees, the need for and practice of EP continues to grow. Regardless of public attitudes toward executive protection, many factors keep the need for EP at a high level: widespread ill will toward highly-paid executives, increasing executive travel around the globe (to participate in emerging markets), ongoing threats from activists and terrorists, and the ease with which potential adversaries can locate executives and discover detailed information about them. (See accompanying box, "Political Violence Against Americans, 2008.")

EP is needed now more than ever, and EP programs are relying on intelligent, leading-edge techniques to provide protection when and where it is needed, in a cost-effective and under-the-radar style.

Political Violence Against Americans, 2008

In 2008, 36 violent incidents around the globe are believed to have resulted from intentional targeting of Americans.

The following findings were developed based on the latest data from the Bureau of Diplomatic Security, U.S. Department of State (*Political Violence Against Americans 2008*):

Geographic Area	Number of Incidents	Number of Americans Killed	Number of Americans Injured
Western Hemisphere	5	0	1
Europe	6	0	0
Sub-Saharan Africa	5	2	0
Near East	16	0	16
South and Central Asia	11	20	31
East Asia and the Pacific	1	0	0

The incidents in which no Americans were injured were typically acts of violence against property, such as car bombs, or else unsuccessful but serious attacks against American citizens themselves.

Note: these figures count only incidents in which Americans were targeted simply because they were Americans—solely politically motivated attacks. Attacks that are not politically motivated affect a much greater number of American victims each year. These include attacks against victims who are chosen because they are economically attractive targets or representatives of disfavored companies.

This book's purpose is threefold:

- To provide security directors with the latest trends and techniques in executive protection so they can protect their organization's top tier executives (including determining whether and how much protection is needed)

- To update EP specialists on the same trends and techniques so they can perform their jobs better
- To attract newcomers to the field of EP in order to improve the security of companies' top personnel assets

The intended audience consists of the following:

- Security directors or chief security officers who oversee (or perhaps should develop) EP programs in their organizations
- EP managers and specialists who wish to boost their knowledge so they can perform their work more effectively
- Security, law enforcement, and other personnel who may wish to consider entering the field of EP

Readers new to this subject may think of the U.S. Secret Service when they consider executive protection. The Secret Service does indeed provide EP service, and it does so at a highly professional level. However, the legal, financial, and material resources of the USSS vastly outweigh those of private-sector EP operations. (For example, a corporate EP program cannot redirect air traffic or close runways for flight security, close public streets for motorcade missions, or seal off whole floors of hotels.) Private-sector EP managers must operate within the same legal framework as other private citizens and tend to have much more limited budgets than the USSS. Therefore, this book focuses mainly on the private-sector EP manager or specialist, who must protect a principal without the vast resources that govment protection agencies have at their disposal.

Regarding nomenclature, in the field of executive protection, the person to be protected is generally called the executive, principal, or protectee. The person providing the protection may be called an EP manager (if the person is in charge of a multi-person EP program) or an EP specialist (if the person is performing the actual tasks of executive protection). This book will use the title EP manager when emphasizing managerial responsibilities and will apply the term EP specialist when emphasizing operational protective responsibilities. In practice, the two job descriptions overlap. Many EP managers perform operational duties as needed, and many EP specialists play some managerial or supervisory role.

This book focuses on private-sector EP specialists, who must protect their principals without government's vast resources and powers.

This book is the third in a series of EP treatments by the author. The reader may find it helpful to understand how the three books fit together.

Book 1

The first book in this series, *The Art of Executive Protection* (Baltimore, Maryland: Noble House, 1997) was carefully designed to address both the EP specialist and the executive. It aimed to provide both the provider and the user of executive protection with a common understanding of what the undertaking involves, what underlies it philosophically, and how it should proceed. When the user and the provider understand executive protection in the same way, the tensions that result from the unknown are reduced, and together the EP specialist and the executive can deploy their resources in the most effective manner.

The book lays out the basics of EP: threat or risk assessment, the philosophy of protection (with six key principles), working the principal (close-in protection), the advance, automobile security, home and office security, domestic and international travel, workplace violence, protection resources, and issues of personnel and training.

The book's foreword was contributed by someone who knows the importance of EP—and the consequences of an EP breach—better than most people: James L. Dozier, MGEN, USA Retired. In 1981 at his home in Verona, Italy, General Dozier was kidnapped by the murderous Red Brigade terrorist organization. At the time of his abduction, General Dozier was the highest-ranking officer in NATO's Southern European Command's LANDSOUTH headquarters. His rescue 42 days later signaled the beginning of the end of the terrorist movement in Italy.

The Art of Executive Protection, now in its fifth printing, presents the timeless fundamentals of executive protection and continues to be an essential reference.

Book 2

Executive Protection: New Solutions for a New Era (Baltimore, Maryland: Noble House, 2006) examines the EP topics that changed the most after the September 11, 2001, terror attacks against the United States. Those terrible events brought security into the spotlight like never before, and interest in executive protection rose to new heights.

The book expands on the basic and advanced concepts of executive protection, adapting them to the post-9/11 era and updating them to reflect developments in global trade, international travel, corporate responsibility, and advanced technologies.

After examining threat trends, the book discusses the practical value of EP in a corporate environment, new techniques in risk assessment, real attacks against executives by various means, countersurveillance, the roles of firearms and technology in EP, and other vital topics. (As a bonus, the book provides sample checklists for conducting advances, which readers may also download from www.rloatman.com.) The focus is primarily on the protection of corporate executives, but it also addresses protection of wealthy private families and of government officials who do not have a full protective detail.

Book 3 (this book)

Executive Protection: Rising to the Challenge is based on the author's continuing, up-to-the-minute experience in providing operational protection, EP risk assessment, or both to many of the largest companies and wealthiest families in the United States, as well as quasigovernmental agencies. The book also shares knowledge he has gained and refined in training the EP personnel of many of the world's largest corporations—at their corporate headquarters and at training programs held around the United States and abroad. It aims to share leading-edge techniques that the best EP managers are employing to protect their principals in ways that are both effective and acceptable in the corporate environment.

Here is what readers can look forward to in this volume:

- **Chapter 2: EP Needed As Never Before** takes a high-level look at the need for executive protection. It assembles a sobering list of attacks and threat trends, examines the latest academic research on the costly impact of attacks, and proposes a practical approach to keeping principals safe in a threatening and rapidly changing world.
- **Chapter 3: Risk Assessment** examines the all-

important basis of executive protection: the level and type of risk faced by the principal. Every discussion of EP must address risk assessment, which is the foundation on which an EP program is built. Chapter 3 offers a case study describing the near-impossibility of devising an EP program without first conducting a thorough risk assessment. It examines the use of risk assessments to defend EP spending and the advantage of using a risk assessment to devise long-term security solutions instead of being whipsawed by daily news events. The chapter also looks at one of the most notorious risks to principals, kidnapping. Ongoing risk assessment is essential for ensuring that an EP program remains focused on the efforts that are needed most.

- **Chapter 4: Intelligence in Executive Protection** differentiates actionable intelligence from mere information and describes the process for generating or otherwise obtaining solid intelligence. The chapter then provides insights into understanding a threat environment and provides a detailed example of how live, "pushed" intelligence served EP details during an actual urban crisis overseas.

- **Chapter 5: Protecting the Reluctant Principal** addresses a common challenge: how to safeguard an executive who prefers not to be surrounded by—or even be much aware of—EP specialists or security measures, even though he or she faces a level of risk that warrants some level of personal protection. The chapter presents various techniques for masking protection and safeguarding principals through the most streamlined, efficient means available.

- **Chapter 6: The Attack Vector** describes a geometrically practical way of looking at, and interrupting, a close-quarters attack against a principal. It applies the EP concept of countersurveillance to close-in protection. It then maps out the pros and cons of different arrangements of EP specialists around a principal in relatively high-risk settings.

- **Chapter 7: Working with Foreign Security Providers** explains why and when an EP program might need to retain assistance from local security professionals to protect a principal traveling outside his or her home country. In addition, the chapter describes how to spot and avoid pitfalls in finding providers, investigating their credentials and capabilities, and establishing fees. Also addressed are issues related to relationship building, management, and supervision, as well as what to look for when seeking to hire security contractors with specific skill sets.

- **Chapter 8: Emergency Extraction of the Principal,** after acknowledging that global business responsibilities can place executives in dangerous settings, describes the many steps an EP manager should take to prepare for and execute a quick, unscheduled removal of the principal from a location that has become too dangerous to remain in (or from a place in which the principal cannot obtain satisfactory medical care for an acute condition). In other words, if the protectee needs to escape a hot spot fast, how can the EP specialist make that happen?

- **Chapter 9: Human Factor: Training and Partnerships** examines two particular personnel issues. It begins by discussing the value of EP staff training, noting sources of training, and listing key topics that should be taught. It then examines (1) partnerships that the EP manager should form within his or her company (embracing travel, business continuity/crisis management, and human resources), and (2) partnerships outside the EP manager's company (mainly with law enforcement).

- **Chapter 10: The Future of Executive Protection** looks at what tools and techniques lie ahead in the practice of EP. In particular, the chapter discusses possible future EP ramifications of technologies for tracking, data collection and management, and facial recognition.

- In the **Afterword**, the author wraps up the book's analysis. He also takes a look at the career of executive protection, remarking on its exciting challenges, significant stakes, and rewarding satisfactions.

- The **Appendix** features a model matrix designed for matching EP measures to varying risk levels. It is designed to be a tool that readers can customize to fit their own security needs and resources. (The matrix file can also be downloaded at www.rloatman.com/book for ease of tailoring.) The author's corporate EP clients have found the matrix to be a helpful tool for quickly adjusting the level of EP service provided to principals as risk levels shift up and down.

- The book concludes with an **Index** for ease of locating key topics.

Many chapters begin with a "tale from the field," that is, a brief case study, based on the author's experience, provided to illustrate key points. Identifying details have been removed to protect the parties involved, but all other important aspects are true to life.

2.

EP Needed As Never Before

Times are harsh. Animosity and overt threats against executives, wealthy families, celebrities, federal judges, and others have surged to a level not seen in years. Evidence is all around.

Terrible Tenor

The following examples show anti-executive behavior, in the United States and Europe, at varying levels of aggressiveness:

- **Threats against Wall Street executives.** As many news accounts note, public animosity toward business executives can rise to surprising levels:[1]

---

[1] Andrew Pergam, "Threats to AIG: 'We Will Get Your Children,'" *NBC Connecticut*, March 26, 2009. Available:
http://www.nbcconnecticut.com/news/local/AIG-Threats-We-will-

The anger in the threats against AIG executives is palpable. "Get the bonus, we will get your children," someone identified only as "Jacob the Killer" hauntingly writes in an e-mail.

Perhaps feeding the frenzy, the reporter then printed disturbing, violent excerpts from nine of the worst threats, adding that protests had taken place at the homes of some AIG employees and that executives in Connecticut were said to have hired security firms to guard their homes.

- **Direct attacks on executives' homes.** Aggrieved parties have been taking their fight not only to the offices of organizations with which they disagree, but also to those organizations' leaders:[2]

> Anti-capitalists today claimed responsibility for vandalizing the home of disgraced former Royal Bank of Scotland boss Sir Fred Goodwin. Several windows in the ex-RBS chief executive's luxury villa in Edinburgh were smashed and a Mercedes in the driveway damaged early this morning.... A group calling themselves Bank Bosses Are Criminals later claimed responsibility and ominously warned the attack was only the start of a campaign against executives. "We are angry that rich people like him are paying themselves a huge amount of money, and living in luxury, while ordinary people are made unemployed, destitute and homeless," the protesters said in an e-mail sent to media organisations. "This is a crime. Bank bosses should be

---

get-your-children.html [2009, June 27].

[2] Nicola Boden, "Anti-Capitalists Admit Attacking Fred the Shred's Home and Warn Other Bankers: 'This is just the beginning,'" *Mail Online*, March 25, 2009. Available: http://www.dailymail.co.uk/news/article-1164691/Fat-cats-terror-anti-capitalists-attack-Fred-Shreds-home.html [2009, June 2]. A follow-up article the next day was titled "Fat Cats in Terror after Anti-Capitalists Attack Fred the Shred's Home."

jailed. This is just the beginning...." Friends are said to have advised [Sir Goodwin] to leave Britain for a few months until public anger dies down. He is also believed to have taken his two children out of school temporarily last year due to fears for their safety.

- **Threats against judges.** Long at risk because of the nature of their work, federal judges are seeing a spike in threats against them and their families:[3]

  Threats against the nation's judges and prosecutors have sharply increased, prompting hundreds to get 24-hour protection from armed U.S. marshals. Many federal judges are altering their routes to work, installing security systems at home, shielding their addresses by paying bills at the courthouse or refraining from registering to vote. Some even pack weapons on the bench.

  The problem has become so pronounced that a high-tech "threat management" center recently opened in Crystal City, where a staff of about 25 marshals and analysts monitor a 24-hour number for reporting threats, use sophisticated mapping software to track those being threatened and tap into a classified database linked to the FBI and CIA.

  "I live with a constant heightened sense of aware-ness," said John R. Adams, a federal judge in Ohio who began taking firearms classes after a federal judge's family was slain in Chicago and takes a pis-tol to the courthouse on weekends. "If I'm going to carry a firearm, I'd better know how to use it."

  The threats and other harassing communications

---

[3] Jerry Markon, "Threats to Judges, Prosecutors Soaring," *The Washington Post*, May 25, 2009, p. A1. Available: http://www.washingtonpost.com/wp-dyn/content/article/2009/05/24/AR2009052402931_pf.html [2009, May 26].

against federal court personnel have more than doubled in the past six years, from 592 to 1,278, according to the U.S. Marshals Service....

The threats are emerging in cases large and small, on the Internet, by telephone, in letters and in person. In the District, two men have pleaded not guilty to charges of vowing to kill a federal prosecutor and kidnap her adult son if she didn't drop a homicide investigation. The judge in the CIA leak case got threatening letters when he ordered Vice President Richard B. Cheney's former chief of staff to prison. A man near Richmond was charged with mailing threats to a prosecutor over three traffic offenses. The face of a federal judge in the District was put in a rifle's cross hairs on the Internet after he issued a controversial environmental ruling, judicial sources said.

- **Widespread mockery over use of private aircraft.** Headlines and media commentary harshly criticized the CEOs of General Motors, Ford, and Chrysler for using corporate aircraft to travel to Washington, DC, to request financial assistance from taxpayers. Then-GM CEO Rick Wagoner's Gulfstream IV[4]

  is just one of a fleet of luxury jets owned by GM that continues to ferry executives around the world despite the company's dire financial straits. "This is a slap in the face of taxpayers," said Tom Schatz, President of Citizens Against Government Waste. "To come to Washington on a corporate jet, and asking for a handout is outrageous." Wagoner's private jet trip to Washington cost his ailing company an estimated $20,000 roundtrip. In compari-

---

[4] Brian Ross and Joseph Rhee, "Big Three CEOs Flew Private Jets to Plead for Public Funds: Auto Industry Close to Bankruptcy But They Get Pricey Perk," *ABC News*, November 19, 2008. Available: http://abcnews.go.com/Blotter/WallStreet/story?id=6285739&page=1 [2008, November 19].

son, seats on Northwest Airlines flight 2364 from Detroit to Washington were going online for $288 coach and $837 first class.

- **Anti-business riots.** In some quarters, ire over business executives' role in economic setbacks has boiled over into actual riots:[5]

  Chanting G-20 protesters clashed with riot police in central London..., overwhelming police lines, vandalizing the Bank of England and smashing windows at the Royal Bank of Scotland. An effigy of a banker was set ablaze, drawing cheers.... [S]ome 4,000 anarchists, anti-capitalists, environmentalists and others clogged London's financial district.... A battered effigy of a banker in a bowler's hat hung on a traffic light near the Bank of England.... Bankers have been lambasted as being greedy and blamed for the recession that is making jobless ranks soar. Other banners read "Banks are evil" and "Eat the bankers".... Some bankers went to work in casual wear Wednesday fearing they could be targeted.... A particularly ferocious balaclava-wearing mob broke into a closed RBS bank branch and stole keyboards, using them to break windows. Other protesters spray-painted graffiti on the RBS building, writing "Class War" and "Thieves." Mounted riot police eventually pushed them back.

- **Domestic terrorism.** An organization need not be the main focus of an extremist movement to be targeted. Even companies that are suspected of doing business with controversial companies may be the object of an attack:[6]

---

[5] Raphael G. Satter, "Protesters Clash with Police at Bank of England," Associated Press, *Washington Post*, April 1, 2009.

[6] Terry Frieden, "Animal Rights Activist on FBI's 'Most Wanted Terrorists' List," *CNN.com*, April 21, 2009. Available:

The FBI for the first time has placed an animal rights activist on the bureau's "Most Wanted Terrorists" list.... Authorities allege [the bomber, Daniel Andreas San Diego] bombed facilities in Emeryville and Pleasanton, California, because he believed the Chiron and Shaklee Corporations had ties to animal-testing labs. The sophisticated homemade bombs had ammonium nitrate brand explosives and relied on "kitchen timer style mechanical timer devices," according to an FBI affidavit. After both bombings, e-mails from a group called "The Revolutionary Cells-Liberation Brigade" claimed responsibility for the acts.

Reports suggest that at the first location, two bombs exploded an hour apart (a common technique for injuring emergency responders), and at the second location the bomb was packed with nails (a technique used to increase injury to persons). He was put on the terrorist list because his actions "have set an example to other extremists in the animal rights movement," the FBI said.

- **Negative news focus on individual executives.** Many recent news stories have singled out corporate executives by name, rather than focusing on their companies. A lead story at FoxNews.com ran prominent, close-up photos of the CEOs of Goldman Sachs, GM, and Merrill Lynch with the caption "THE BAD APPLES: As bailout USA rumbles on, take a look at the schools where American's 'captains of industry' got their training before they ran their corporate ships aground."[7] The photo links to a list of 39 top corporate

---

http://www.cnn.com/2009/CRIME/04/21/fbi.domestic.terror.suspect/index.html [2009, April 27].

[7] "The Bad Apples," *FoxNews.com*, February 17, 2009. Available:

executives, including where they attended undergraduate and graduate school and when they graduated. The article includes photos of about half the executives, giving the impression of a target list.

- **Hostage-taking by employees, tolerated by police.** In early 2009, French employees of three corporations held executives hostage because of labor grievances. Executives or managers of Sony, Caterpillar, and 3M were all held captive for one or more days by disgruntled employees. Some executive hostage-takings have gone on for five days.

  Hostage-taking by employees is not always condemned, even by authorities:[8]

  > 'Boss-napping falls into a particular category,' says French police spokesman Laurent Bischoff. 'Technically, it amounts to kidnapping, but it's not regarded as an offense.' Police rarely intervene.... Riot police did turn up in Paris on Tuesday when angry employees of luxury-goods company PPR SA besieged a taxi carrying CEO François-Henri Pinault. Police dispersed the workers, but Mr. Bischoff says that was 'because they blocked traffic.'

  Could executive hostage-taking spread? A common view among various specialists in such matters is that it could. Aside from France, cases have recently been reported in Britain and Slovakia. David Partner, a kidnap and ransom expert at Miller Insurance, an insurance broker affiliated with Lloyd's of London, says, "Be-

---

http://www.foxnews.com/story/0,2933,494445,00.html [2009, February 17].

[8] David Gauthier-Villars and Leila Abboud, "In France, the Bosses Can Become Hostages," *Wall Street Journal* on-line, April 3, 2009. Available: http://online.wsj.com/article/SB123871251471484469.html [2009, April 3].

cause of the state of the world economy, it would not surprise me if bosses were held hostage by workers more frequently."[9] Gary Chaison, a professor of industrial relations at Clark University in Massachusetts, notes, "I could easily see executive hostage-taking happening [in the United States] within a few months."[10]

- **Extreme comments by government figures.** Iowa Senator Charles Grassley said AIG executives should[11]

    follow the Japanese example and come before the American people and take that deep bow and say, I'm sorry, and then either do one of two things: resign or go commit suicide. And in the case of the Japanese, they usually commit suicide before they make any apology.

    He later softened his remarks, but his comment illustrates the high level of animosity toward corporate executives and the apparent acceptability of threatening remarks.

- **Gratuitous harassment of executives.** Recently a top executive of a major public corporation (a client of the author) was repeatedly shouted at and denigrated in several New England towns while on vacation, solely because he drove an expensive car and spent freely in stores.

Signs of ill will and danger appear throughout the culture. A recent cover of *The Economist* features the Eugène Delacroix painting *Liberty Leading the People*, which depicts Lady Liberty bearing a musket with bayonet while dead royalists lie at her

---

[9] "Kidnapped," *The Economist*, March 21, 2009, p. 68.
[10] Ibid.
[11] "Iowa Senator Says AIG Executives Should 'Resign or Commit Suicide,'" *FoxNews.com*, March 16, 2009, www.foxnews.com.

feet upon the barricades—but in the magazine's version, she is also holding a banner that reads "GET THE RICH!"[12]

To anyone charged with protecting corporate executives or members of wealthy families (generally called "principals"), public antipathy matters greatly. The same threats that principals have always faced remain, but the hostile civic mood draws out abusive behavior from a much wider swath of the public, even if that behavior does not always rise to the level of attempted murder. To serve their principals well and help them remain focused on their priorities, EP specialists must protect them not only from violent attacks but also from lower-level harassment that impedes their ability to travel and work efficiently. In other words, actual heckling, obnoxious phone calls, and home vandalism can distract and disable a principal as much as, or even more than, the less visible, non-executed threat of kidnapping by professional criminals.

> **EP specialists protect against both violent attacks and lower-level harassment that impedes principals in their work.**

At the same time that EP is needed as never before, some corporations are displaying a hesitancy to expend the necessary resources. Not only are they facing financial constraints related to worldwide economic trends, but they also appear to fear public or shareholder backlash against any spending that looks like special treatment for executives. For example, public criticism of GM's, Chrysler's, and Ford's use of private aircraft for its executives reached a peak just when those executives most

---

12 *The Economist*, April 4-10, 2009. It is worth noting that the painting depicts France's July 1830 Revolution, in which one monarch (Charles X) was overthrown but immediately replaced with another (Louis-Philippe).

needed the extra protection that private air travel can afford. The combination of a high level of need for EP and a low level of willingness to spend money on it creates a serious challenge for security professionals tasked with EP responsibilities, as well as for the executives themselves.

Costly Impact of Attacks

It has long been clear that a successful attack against a corporate principal is costly in many ways. Even if the principal survives the attack, he or she may be too distracted to work efficiently for some time or may choose to leave the organization and head to safer ground.

What has always been less clear is the large-scale cost to the corporation in terms of lost stock value. Fortunately, research by a pair of finance scholars from Ohio State University and Purdue University quantifies the losses that corporations can expect when their personnel or facilities are attacked by terrorists.[13]

Professors Karolyi and Martell summarize their study methodology and findings as follows:

> This paper examines the stock price impact of terrorist attacks. Using an official list of terrorism-related incidents compiled by the Counterterrorism Office of the U.S. Department of State, we identify 75 attacks between 1995 and 2002 in which publicly traded firms are targets. An event-study analysis around the day of the attacks uncovers evidence of a statistically significant negative stock price reaction of -0.83%, which corresponds to an average loss per firm per attack of $401 million in firm market capitalization. A cross sectional analysis of the abnormal returns in-

---

[13] G. Andrew Karolyi and Rodolfo Martell, "Terrorism and the Stock Market," unpublished research awaiting review, 2006. Available: http://papers.ssrn.com/sol3/papers.cfm?abstract_id=823465 [2009, April 7].

dicates that the impact of terrorist attacks differs according to the home country of the target firm and the country in which the incident occurred. Attacks in countries that are wealthier and more democratic are associated with larger negative share price reactions. Most interestingly, we find that human capital losses, such as kidnappings of company executives, are associated with larger negative stock price reactions than physical losses, such as bombings of facilities or buildings.... The stock price reactions are not reversed within our window of analysis [the seven-year period studied].

The researchers go on to offer these potential explanations for the drop in share price:

Price changes might reflect updated market beliefs that the attacks change firms' investment policies, that the company is forced into higher security costs, and [that] future cash flows [will be lost] due to direct asset losses. In other words, the stock price effect should reflect the fact that costs incurred by the firm in the continuation of its normal activities differ from those before the attack(s). Alternatively, the stock price reaction could also reflect an increased likelihood of a future attack, since the firm has already been revealed to have the attention of at least one terrorist group.

What are the key points for an EP specialist to draw from this study? Here are a few:

- After a terrorist attack against a company's personnel or facilities, the company's stock price may be expected to drop 0.83 percent.
- That price drop is likely to last for years.
- The share price drop is greater for attacks that take place in countries that are "wealthier and more democratic."
- Attacks against personnel lead to greater stock price declines than attacks against facilities.

- The average corporate loss ($401 million) greatly exceeds any amount that could ever have been spent on the security measures that might have prevented the attack.

Not all attacks against corporate executives are committed by terrorists in the usual sense of that word. For example, an executive could be harmed by a disgruntled employee or a mentally ill attention-seeker. Moreover, sometimes top executives die unexpectedly from natural causes (such as heart attacks) or accidents (such as fires or vehicle crashes). The research by Karolyi and Martell did not examine the impact of such events, but those other causes of death are also among the traditional concerns of EP specialists, who aim to preserve their principals from all causes of harm, so their impact must be examined as well.

Fortunately, other academics have examined the financial implications of sudden executive deaths due to accidents or sudden illnesses. In "An Analysis of the Stock Price Reaction to Sudden Executive Deaths: Implications for the Managerial Labor Market,"[14] researchers from Northwestern University, the University of Pittsburgh, and the University of Michigan discovered a complex relationship between causes of death (illness or accident), the executive's status as a founder or non-founder of the company, and share prices after the executive's death. A key finding for EP specialists is that the accidental (not illness-related) death of a non-founding executive adversely affected a company's share prices by 0.83 percent—the same

---

[14] W. Bruce Johnson, Robert P. Magee, Nandu J. Nagarajan, and Harry A. Newman, "An Analysis of the Stock Price Reaction to Sudden Executive Deaths: Implications for the Managerial Labor Market," *Journal of Accounting and Economics*, April 1985, pp. 151-174. Available: http://deepblue.lib.umich.edu/bitstream/2027.42/25717/1/000027 4.pdf [2009, April 9].

level as found in the Karolyi study on terrorist attack effects conducted some 12 years later.

Taken together, the two studies suggest that terrorist attacks against corporate personnel and facilities, and fatal accidents involving corporate executives, lead to substantial, lasting losses in corporate share prices, easily equating to hundreds of millions of dollars.

Balancing the cost of providing executive protection against the enormous losses that the service may prevent, and weighing the positive benefits of executive protection as well, many companies have concluded that EP provides a positive return on investment. The image below represents that conclusion graphically.

Balancing the cost of EP against losses avoided and positive benefits, many companies find EP provides a good return on investment

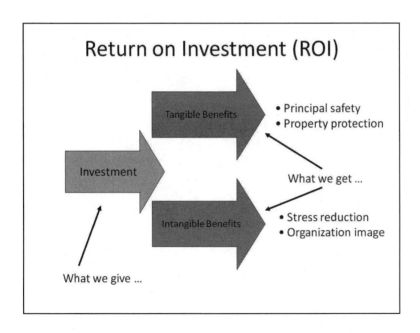

A Way Out

As the preceding sections have demonstrated, today's top corporate executives face high levels of risk from many quarters. Moreover, the potential losses resulting from a successful attack against a principal can be highly significant. In addition, sentiment among shareholders, the media, and the government is not necessarily favorable to large-scale, highly visible EP operations. Nevertheless, many executives urgently need protection. Fortunately, EP managers can provide the necessary level of protection through thoughtful measures to safeguard the principal without fanning the flames of outsiders' resentment. They can satisfy their companies' and principals' needs through the leading-edge techniques presented in this book.

Executive protection is a zero defects field. One mistake can be a calamity.

To make the best use of the specific guidance in this book, an EP manager may wish to keep a certain phrase in mind: *zero defects*. The term refers to a business concept that was popular recently and that can be profitably applied to executive protection.

EP is different from other security disciplines. In retail theft prevention, a security program can be considered successful even if a small number of thefts continue to take place. In the financial services industry, a security program is expected to minimize fraud losses, but no one expects all losses to be prevented.

Executive protection, by contrast, is a zero defects field. If even one serious attack succeeds against a protected executive, the protection program cannot be considered a true success. One mistake can be a calamity. Perhaps like airline bomb screening, EP's job is to utterly prevent low-likelihood, high-consequence events. It is not every day that an adversary attacks the protectee, but if the adversary does—and succeeds—the result is disaster. Clearly, the EP program has to aim for zero defects.

The zero defects approach—doing it right the first time and every time—is hard work, but it can pay off. In most businesses, the goal of the zero defects approach is to increase the employer's profits by

- eliminating the costs that result from failure and
- increasing revenues through increased customer satisfaction.

In executive protection, the zero defects model has two similar aims:

- to avoid mistakes and completely prevent successful attacks against a protectee and
- to use protection measures that help, not harm, the principal's working conditions and quality of life.

Zero defects, in the EP context, means never letting the principal travel without advance notice of the risks and resources at the destination; never allowing the principal to walk into high-risk situations without protection; and never dropping the ball on the seemingly mundane responsibilities of EP, such as keeping cars gassed up and ready to go, checking the principal's mail for potential hazards, etc. It also means using resources in the most effective manner possible, such as maximizing training to get the most out of the EP program's personnel.

In executive protection, success in the zero defects approach creates a virtuous cycle—not a vicious cycle, but a beneficial one. (See following box.)

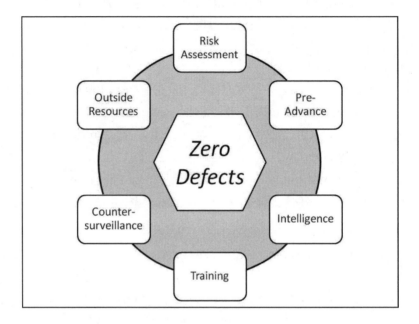

The better an EP program performs its duties, the more professional and less obtrusive it will seem to the principal, and hence the more protection the principal will accept in his or her life.

3.
Risk Assessment

Tale from the Field

A high-profile international political figure, who had recently returned to private-citizen status after completing a term of elective office, faced a sky-high level of risk. He had left the Islamic faith of his childhood and begun to speak and write about his disagreement with some of its tenets and customs. In response, he was placed under a fatwa (decree of an Islamic religious leader) calling for his death. He moved to a new country, and benefactors funded a protection effort to keep him safe.

However, he and his protection team found themselves frustrated. They both felt uncertain about what protective measures were appropriate and how to carry them out in a manner convenient to the principal's life style. Repeatedly, they tried restructuring the protection program, but the arrangement still seemed rudderless and unsatisfactory.

The principal's benefactors called on the author's firm to redesign the protection program. The author pointed out that unless a serious, formal risk assessment is conducted first, an EP program is unlikely to succeed. Without knowing the risks, it is impossible to know what protection measures are needed. The risk assessment tells the principal or the EP staff what the specific risk profile is and what security measures can help reduce those risks.

The benefactors said they already knew the principal faced a high risk, so a risk assessment would be a waste of time. However, designing an EP program without first conducting a risk assessment is like building a house without an architect or blueprints. The builder may decide an architect is too expensive and simply unnecessary; since the builder has constructed homes in the past, why spend the money? The outcome is that the house does not properly fit the hilly site, it does not meet the owner's needs, the contractors become frustrated, and the budget spirals out of control.

To change the comparison, a risk assessment becomes a road map, clarifying where to go and therefore what to do. That road map is then based not on guesses or assumptions but on facts and insights gained from on-the-ground interviews.

In this case, without a risk assessment, the principal and his protectors were doomed to repeated frustration.

As Chapter 1 observed, every discussion of executive protection must address risk assessment, the necessary foundation of an EP program. This book is no exception, and neither were its two predecessors. This time, however, the emphasis is on several benefits and applications of risk assessments that may have been less evident in the past.

To set the stage, this chapter first summarizes the core components of an EP risk assessment. Next comes a look at an important secondary use for risk assessments—not just creating a blueprint for the EP program but also quantitatively justifying the very existence of the program. The chapter then examines a useful way of viewing risk assessments—as tools for creating protective visions rather than for generating point-by-point checklists of risks and countermeasures. The chapter concludes by demonstrating one way of applying risk assessment to the threat of kidnapping, a type of attack that many people particularly dread.

Components of Risk Assessment

In a risk assessment, one identifies the risks facing the principal so that those risks can be mitigated through realistic recommendations geared toward achievable results.

Premise

An EP program has a finite sum of protective resources, such as money, personnel, influence, knowledge, and contacts. Collectively, an EP program's resources should be allocated toward preventing the threats that present the greatest possibility of harm; it would not make sense to divide the resources evenly among the entire pool of conceivable threats.

To allocate EP resources wisely, then, it is necessary to ascertain, to the degree possible, the likelihood and impact of

various potential threats, based on
the principal's activities and identity.
The risk assessment is the tool for
studying the range of threats, likelihood of victimization, and impact of
successful attacks against a principal.
With the information the risk assessment generates, the EP program
can begin to prioritize the dangers
against which the principal should be

> **Risk assessment is the tool for studying the range of threats, likelihood of victimization, and impact of successful attacks against a principal.**

protected and then devise appropriate protective measures.

Range of Threats

Prominent executives may face a wide range of potential
threats. The following list is not exhaustive, but it represents
more than enough danger to keep an EP program busy:

- Assassination
- Kidnapping
- Street violence
- Attacks by insane persons or zealots
- Workplace violence
- Terrorist attacks
- Embarrassment (deliberate or accidental)
- Injury (unintentional)
- Illness or medical emergency
- That which is least expected

Few principals face a high risk from all those threats at once.
To determine which threats apply to a particular principal (and
under what circumstances), the EP manager can analyze them
through the process of risk analysis, described below.

Risk Analysis

In this framework, risk analysis is a particular step within the larger process of risk assessment. Risk analysis is nothing mysterious, but it is a rigorous task. It consists of the careful collection and examination of data to determine the scope, severity, likelihood, impact, and other characteristics of particular hazards. To make risk analysis as effective as possible, the EP manager should strive not to overlook any hazards or other relevant factors, should obtain updated data continually, and should analyze the information in an organized way.

One way to perform a risk analysis is to ask the traditional reporter's questions: who, what, when, where, and why. In each of those categories, different specific queries are appropriate for different principals. In general, however, the right types of questions are these:

- Who am I protecting (corporate executive, government official, celebrity, wealthy person, controversial activist)?

- What must I protect the principal from (mugging, embarrassment, kidnapping, harassment, stalking, accidental injury, assassination, heart attack)?

- When must I protect the principal (eight hours a day, 24 hours a day)?

- Where must I protect the principal (at work, at home, while commuting, while traveling)?

- Why must I protect the principal (to preserve privacy or life, protect corporation's leading human asset, facilitate safe movement near and far)?

Risk analysis, then, is the discovery and examination of data about possible threats to the principal. Risk assessment uses the results of risk analysis to paint an overall picture of the principal's level of risk and begin to form or modify an EP program.

Some people cringe when they hear the U.S. Constitution described as a living document, but EP managers know their risk assessment must indeed be a living document, regularly changing to reflect shifting conditions in the world. If something increases the principal's level of risk, then the risk assessment must change, as must the protective measures provided by the EP program.

EP Program Justification

An EP risk assessment is, as has been observed, necessary for the proper allocation of EP resources and effective design of an EP program. However, the presence or absence of an EP risk assessment may have other ramifications as well.

With a Risk Assessment

With a thorough, up-to-date risk assessment, an EP program can attempt to apply some quantitative values to the risks and potential losses that an EP program can reduce. In this context, likelihood times impact equals the level of threat and theoretically the amount of money one should be willing to spend to eliminate that threat. EP risk assessment is not mathematically precise, but it does attempt to quantify the hazards a principal faces and the costs of EP incidents to create a general, realistic basis for designing and funding an EP program. (Chapter 2, EP Needed As Never Before, provides a research-supported basis for estimating the harm that can follow a successful attack against a principal.) With a proper risk assessment, an EP program can not only allocate its resources most effectively but also justify the program's existence and budget.

Without a Risk Assessment

Without a formal risk assessment, not only does an EP program face frustration and inefficiency in applying its energies, but it also may be left with little convincing defense when its budget is attacked. If the risk level to a principal cannot be shown (by a risk assessment) to warrant a dedicated EP program, then having such a program may cast the principal and the organization in a bad light, especially during a time of

Without a formal risk assessment, an EP program faces frustration and inefficiency and may have little defense when its budget is attacked.

cost-cutting. A recent news article illustrates the way an EP program may appear if it is based only on gut feelings, a vague sense that other organizations are operating similar programs, or the mere fact that the program has been in existence for years:[15]

> Montgomery County [Maryland] Executive Ike Leggett's proposed budget would pay his four bodyguards an average of $90,000 a year in salary and benefits.
>
> With the county facing unprecedented budget deficits of more than $520 million, some County Council members are questioning whether lower-paid guards could be used. And one councilman is questioning whether Leggett needs a security detail at all.
>
> "I've just always asked myself whether such a security detail was required for anyone in that position," said Council Vice President Roger Berliner, D-Potomac/Bethesda....

---

[15] Alan Suderman, "Leggett Bodyguards Would Make $90K a Year in Proposed Budget," *The Washington Examiner*, April 19, 2009. Available: http://www.washingtonexaminer.com/local/Leggett-bodyguards-would-make-90K-a-year-in-proposed-budget-43256262.html [2009, April 19].

Assistant Police Chief Drew Tracy said the Beltway sniper attacks in October 2002 prompted the county to assign a security detail for county executives.

Berliner, who sits on the County Council's Public Safety Committee, said he...would like to see Leggett take a look at whether the costs are necessary, especially given the county's budget woes.

Leggett spokesman Patrick Lacefield said...the county government's opinion is that the security detail was a "reasonable precaution," and added that other local elected officials have similar arrangements.

"Is this unusual in the region? I don't think so," Lacefield said.

Prince George's County [Maryland] Executive Jack Johnson's security team is made up of three full-time police officers, according to a police department spokesman.

But across the Potomac [in Virginia], it's a different story.

Alexandria's elected officials have no dedicated security detail, according to a spokesman.

And in Fairfax County, neither the county executive nor any member of the Board of Supervisors, including the chairwoman, have security personnel.

"It's just something we never thought was necessary," Chairwoman Sharon Bulova said.

The Montgomery County government may or may not have conducted a thorough risk assessment to guide and justify the EP program, but the county was (perhaps for perfectly justifiable reasons) unable to produce one at the time the preceding article was being reported. Instead, the county had to rely on fairly vague justifications of the EP program. In another article, the county spokesman offers another non-risk assessment-based justification: the assertion that the cost of the program is too small to be concerned about. Like the other defenses, it is an unconvincing justification of the program:[16]

> [The EP program] costs taxpayers nearly $500,000 a year. "The security detail has been going on for seven years," said…spokesman…Lacefield. "Why should we talk about it?…We just cut $150 million from the budget. We know about cutting spending. This is rather small. It's a nothing burger."

Being able to point to an up-to-date risk assessment, without sharing the details of the assessment, can help justify EP expenditures. Telling the public that half a million dollars is too small to discuss may not be effective. The point is not whether the Montgomery County executive needs EP. Rather, the point is that an organization needs an EP risk assessment, even if its details are not shared, to justify an EP program, both internally and externally.

Toward a Vision, Not a Checklist

Over time, practitioners find new ways to think about and use risk assessments. One angle on risk assessments is to use them not to attempt to predict specific attacks but instead to use risk assessments to understand the big picture regarding the dangers facing a protectee. In other words, a risk assessment may be best applied to macro-level, not micro-level, decision making.

A member of the London Metropolitan Police's Counter Terrorist Command noted the following about risk assessments:[17]

> Rather than dealing solely with threats, we are more inter-

---

[16] Roby Chavez, "County Exec's Security Draws Questions," *My-FoxDC.com*, April 20, 2009. Available: http://www.myfoxdc.com/dpp/news/local/042009_leggetts_security_detail [2009, April 22].

[17] "Critical Protection," *Remploy Frontline*, April 2009.

ested in risks and vulnerabilities.... Our concern will always be to influence companies to change behavior, security measures or business systems.... [I]t is far better if you can sell the idea to the board as a more comprehensive approach to risk management. So, for example, you can offer them measures regarding the vetting of staff, or having systems in place that help with general business continuity-related issues, including terrorism, denial of service, loss of power or loss of key workers.

A good example [of why to employ measures that protect against a continuum of risks rather than focusing on specific threats] would be that on 5 July 2005, the national threat level [in the United Kingdom] had just been lowered and within a 24-hour period terrorists had killed more than 50 people on the London Underground and busses, and injured many more. You can't defend against that kind of unknown quantity. As the former head of MI5, Eliza Manningham-Buller, said, while we had been strategicly aware of the threat, tactically it was a surprise. Our argument is that companies don't want to be learning to dance right before the party.... [A]n intelligence-led but risk-based approach is preferable.

As the Counter Terrorist Command member observes, in general a risk assessment provides a strategic view but not necessarily actionable tactical information. In some cases, an EP manager may be aware of specific threats against a principal or know of a history of certain types of attacks against executives at a location to which the principal is traveling. However, most of the time the risk assessment aids mainly in guiding an EP program to implement a certain level of protective measures. The risk assessment may not be as useful for anticipating or avoiding a particular attack. In other words, EP managers may find it helpful to use the risk assessment to develop an overall protective vision (e.g., setting the EP program to a low, medium, or high pitch of protection), rather than expecting that the risk assessment will point to a specific security measure needed to combat a specific threat. For the executive protection manager, the risk assessment is an effective tool for looking at the big picture from an outsider's perspective.

A Look at Kidnapping

Kidnapping is an especially dreaded form of attack against a principal. A kidnapping incident may be violent, very uncomfortable, expensive, lengthy, injurious, or even fatal. However, for most protectees it is not the likeliest form of attack they may face. Moreover, the risk of kidnapping is not uniform across all the destinations a principal may visit, and not all principals face the same likelihood of being kidnapped at a given place.

Because the risk of kidnapping weighs heavily on some travelers' minds, it is important for the EP manager to take several steps with respect to that threat:

- Assess the likelihood of a kidnapping of the principal based on where he or she lives, works, or travels.

- Assess the likelihood of a kidnapping of the principal based on who he or she is or what the principal represents.

- Explain the various likelihoods to the principal to put him or her on alert at dangerous times and locations and to put the principal more at ease at relatively safe times and locations.

- Devise protective measures appropriate to the risk level at different times and places.

This section shows how a good approach to risk assessment can be applied to the particular risk of kidnapping.

Effect of Location

Location has a very significant impact on the likelihood of kidnapping. In some parts of the world, the crime is rare, while in other places it is extremely common. In assessing the risk of a kidnapping of the principal, the EP manager should first examine the incidence of kidnapping in the specific areas in which the principal works, lives, or travels.

Here is a recent overview of kidnapping around the world, focusing on kidnappings of businesspeople:[18]

> To the sundry costs of doing business abroad, add the risk of abduction. From Mexico to India, Nigeria to Greece, sophisticated gangs are nabbing American workers....

> Kidnapping has become a swelling line item in the global economy. No longer confined to a few dangerous spots in Latin America like Colombia, the nabbing of wealthy individuals and executives has metastasized into a worldwide business. While no international law enforcement agency, like Interpol, keeps tabs, a July report by IKV Pax Christi in Utrecht, Netherlands, says there were 25,000 confirmed kidnappings in 2006. The Dutch nongovernment group guesstimates that there are three unreported cases for every one recorded in a police log. That suggests 100,000 abductions a year. These figures include only cases where the perpetrators are demanding something (and thus exclude child molesting and divorce custody battles).

> Political cases make for big headlines—witness the dramatic rescue this summer of Ingrid Betancourt and three Northrop Grumman contractors held for years by insurgents in the Colombian jungle—but these are not a large fraction of the cases. Behind almost every abduction is a profit motive. It may be an "express" kidnapping, ending in a run to the nearest ATM; sometimes it's a faked abduction, an extortion attempt conducted while the criminal pretends to have a child or spouse in custody. A lot of the time the targets are employees of large corporations that

---

[18] Nathan Vardi, "Kidnap Inc.," *Forbes*, October 13, 2008.

are presumed to have fat wallets. Adobe, Royal Dutch Shell, Chevron, Schlumberger and Halliburton have all suffered kidnappings.

Kidnappings threaten to destabilize entire countries, like Mexico, where the drug cartels pinpoint anyone with money, and Haiti, where petty thugs mark Americans. Guerrillas target oil company workers in Nigeria, pirates ransom cargo ship operators off the coast of Somalia and criminal gangs go after tech executives and their children in India. China's Guangdong Province, teeming with affluent businessmen from Taiwan and Hong Kong, has seen a spike in kidnappings.

The preceding account is frightening reading for an EP manager tasked with protecting principals in high-risk areas. The box on the following page may add to the concern.

The numbers and rates of kidnappings in various countries may be available on-line or from security intelligence sources, and the EP manager should check for the latest details before every trip the principal takes. Of course, for EP purposes, what matters is not only the total number of kidnappings experienced in an area, or even the number of kidnappings per capita. The EP manager should also investigate kidnapping methods in areas where the principal lives, works, or travels.

For many U.S. executives, the closest place they are likely to visit that has a high rate of kidnapping is Latin America, especially Mexico. The author has conducted executive protection training in Mexico City for both U.S. companies operating in that region and Mexican firms and also has conducted security awareness training with U.S. expatriates living in Mexico.

Worldwide Kidnapping 2006

Ranked by estimated number of kidnappings

1. Mexico	8. Venezuela
2. Iraq	9. Colombia
3. India	10. Bangladesh
4. South Africa	11. Nigeria
5. Brazil	12. Haiti
6. Pakistan	13. Afghanistan
7. Ecuador	

Note: China is not included because of a lack of up-to-date figures for 2005 and 2006.

Ranked by estimated number of kidnappings per capita of the population

1. Iraq	7. South Africa
2. Mexico	8. Trinidad & Tobago
3. Chechen Republic	9. Venezuela
4. Ecuador	10. Colombia
5. Brazil	11. India
6. Haiti	

Source: IKV Pax Christi, "Kidnapping Is Booming Business," Utrecht, the Netherlands, 2008. Available: http://www.ikvpaxchristi.nl/files/Documenten/LA%20Colombia/English%20Colombia/Eng%20brochure_Opmaak%201.pdf [2009, April 13].

From an EP perspective, their fear is real and the level of risk is high. The source below describes trends in the execution and resolution of kidnappings in that country:[19]

> Over the last several months there has been an alarming shift in the paradigm that has defined kidnap for ransom cases in Mexico (and the rest of Latin America) for decades. The significance of this shift has been driven home by the recent kidnapping of Felix Batista, an experienced,

---

[19] "Rapidly Changing Kidnapping Threat in Mexico," *Threat Update*, Vehicle Dynamics, January 21, 2009.

highly capable and well-respected anti-kidnapping consultant and negotiator who has managed over 100 kidnapping cases to a successful conclusion.

Further evidence of this shift was presented when authorities announced that a body discovered a few days earlier in Mexico City had been positively identified as that of Silvia Vargas Escalera, the teenaged daughter of a prominent Mexican official that had been kidnapped some fifteen months earlier. In many ways, that case bears a close resemblance to that of Fernando Marti, the fourteen year old son of a wealthy Mexican businessman, whose body was recovered *after* a ransom was negotiated and paid....

[F]urther evidence that the groups responsible for these crimes are attempting to force a change in the way these cases are handled...is a case where the victim's brother-in-law was himself kidnapped and held for ransom when he delivered the agreed upon ransom for the first victim.

The likelihood that the perpetrators...throughout Mexico will increase their efforts to change the dynamics of the negotiation process is exceedingly high.

As the preceding article suggests, in examining the incidence of kidnapping in various countries and cities, the EP manager may need to look beyond raw numbers and consider also the current and evolving techniques of kidnapping in the area.

The risk of kidnapping is relatively low in the United States, but the crime does take place. Because some kidnappings are kept quiet and the FBI does not treat kidnapping as a separate, reportable offense in its Uniform Crime Reports completed by police departments across the nation, it is difficult to estimate the annual number of executive kidnappings in the United States. Whatever the number, executives are indeed kidnapped in the United States; they certainly stand out as lucrative targets to kidnappers who are committing their crimes primarily or solely for the ransom. This leads to the next part of the assessment: looking at the effect not of geography but of the principal's particular identity.

Effect of Principal's Identity

In assessing the risk of a more personally targeted kidnapping—that is, a kidnapping carried out less randomly and more because the principal is visibly affluent, known to be influential, or representative of something the kidnappers dislike—one method is to ask and answer a series of questions such as the following:

- **Does the principal stand out as an attractive target because of wealth?** A principal may give indicators of wealth by flying to a destination on a private aircraft, by travelling around in expensive automobiles, by staying at the highest-end hotels, or by sporting expensive jewelry or clothing. Some principals are named in the *Forbes* lists of wealthy individuals or in similar lists. At least one executive kidnapping in the United States of which the author is aware was facilitated by simple Internet research. The kidnappers were looking for a wealthy person to target; on a *Forbes* list they found one who was listed as living nearby; and then they executed the crime.

- **Does the principal stand out as an attractive target by virtue of representing something the kidnappers dislike?** The principal may represent a company, an industry, a country, a religion, or something else against which the kidnappers hold a grievance.

- **Is the principal highly similar to other people who have been kidnapped?** This is a different way of getting at the same issue as in the preceding question. If other executives working on their business interests in South America have been kidnapped by Marxist guerrillas, it may not be too much of a stretch to conclude that the EP manager's principal may face a significant kidnapping risk if he or she travels there. Likewise, if plant workers in, for example, France have kidnapped or imprisoned executives at company facilities in the past, then a principal who travels to France to conduct labor negotiations may face an elevated risk of similar victimization.

- **Is there a history of threats against the principal?** If the protectee has received threatening letters, e-mails, or phone calls, or if threats against the principal have been made at on-line message boards or blogs, the risk of kidnapping may be elevated.

The research and analysis approach applied here to kidnapping can also be applied to other hazards that principals face, such those listed earlier in the chapter: assassination, street violence, attacks by insane persons or zealots, workplace violence, terrorist attacks, embarrassment (deliberate or accidental), injury (unintentional), and illness or other medical emergency.

Looking back at the story that began this chapter—about the risk assessment that was never started—the executive protection manager has been replaced multiple times, and the protective detail is frustrated and rudderless. The principal has lost confidence and patience. The budget does not support the protective effort, and most important, the risk level continues to be high.

As for the story of the builder who decided not to use an

architect or blueprints, what happened there? After months of delays, budget overruns, and a disappointed homeowner, the house's foundation cracked, the roof caved in, and what was left slid down the mountainside. The owner has to scrap the project and start over.

4.
Intelligence in Executive Protection

Tale from the Field

The following is a news account of the London bombings of July 7, 2005:[20]

Four suicide bombers struck in central London on Thursday 7 July, killing 52 people and injuring more than 770. The co-ordinated attacks hit the transport system as the morning rush hour drew to a close....

Piccadilly line train. The device was next to the rear set of double doors in the front carriage of the train. Twenty-six people, plus the bomber, were killed. More than 340 were injured....

---

[20] "7 July Bombings," *BBC News.* Available: http://news.bbc.co.uk/2/shared/spl/hi/uk/05/london_blasts/what_happened/html/ [2009, June 22].

First Circle line train. The device was placed on the floor at the rear of the second carriage. It killed seven people, plus the bomber, and injured 171, at least 10 seriously.

Second Circle line train. The device was on the floor of the second carriage, close to the forward set of double doors. It killed six people, plus the bomber, and injured 163 others.

Number 30 double-decker bus. It was travelling from Marble Arch to Hackney but had been diverted from its normal route because of road closures in the wake of the tube bombings around an hour earlier.

The bomb, placed on a seat or the floor at the back of the upper deck, killed 13 people, plus the bomber. More than 110 were injured.

The preceding information comes from a summary of the events, compiled after the fact by BBC News. This chapter will examine how the information might have appeared to travelers visiting London on the day of the attack and how good intelligence can support the EP effort. As Mark Twain observed, "It is wiser to find out than to suppose."

Threats to executives are multifaceted and multidimensional, but they come in two general types: intrinsic and dynamic. To maximize the protection of the executive, the EP specialist must understand not only the intrinsic threats posed by the country, city, and neighborhood where business is being conducted, but also the dynamic or event-based threats that may interfere with secure visits, safe meetings, and smooth business dealings.

There is no such thing as a risk-free environment, but a solid and robust intelligence regime can provide the EP specialist with the information and knowledge necessary to minimize the chances that unforeseen threats and hazards will derail the business at hand.

In general parlance the words *risk* and *threat* are often used interchangeably; however, in the professional arena it is useful to draw a clear distinction between the two. In the present context, a threat is any condition, event, or incident that could have a harmful effect on the principal. Risk is the principal's vulnerability to that threat.

For example, declarations from a social activist network that it intends to attack or kidnap executives of pharmaceutical companies visiting London during a major convention would certainly mark an increased threat toward executives. However, if the EP specialist's particular principal will not be in London for the conference, but will instead be working in Philadelphia, his or her level of risk is minimal to nonexistent with regard to the social activist network in London.

The challenge for the EP specialist is to

- identify and qualify the potential threats that could affect the principal,
- understand the risk profile or level of vulnerability the principal has to any given threat, and
- use available data and resources to mitigate, manage, or lessen the degree of risk to the protectee.

The skill most likely to enable the EP specialist to overcome these challenges is the discipline of intelligence. Intelligence is best thought of as a systematic process of gathering information to generate relevant and reliable knowledge. Information that is gained too late or that is inaccurate can end up being as bad or worse than no information at all. Only relevant and reliable knowledge will enable those charged with the protection of executives to take actions that can greatly reduce their vulnerability to risk.

This chapter describes the systematic processes most likely to produce relevant and reliable knowledge. It also offers case studies in which early and accurate intelligence allowed an EP specialist to understand both intrinsic and dynamic threats facing the protectee.

Intelligence Cycle

Intelligence professionals commonly conceive of the intelligence cycle as consisting of five steps: planning, requirements, and direction; collection; analysis and processing; production; and dissemination. The intelligence cycle is a systematic process for generating solid intelligence.

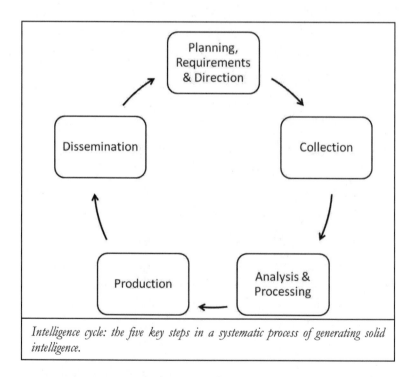

Intelligence cycle: the five key steps in a systematic process of generating solid intelligence.

Planning, Requirements, and Direction

At a high level, the EP specialist's requirement is constantly the same: keeping the principal safe so he or she can work effectively. To make plans toward that end, the EP specialist should ask the following questions:

- What is the principal's destination?
  - What do I know about it?
  - What do I *not* know about it?
- What business is to be conducted?
- What other activities will be undertaken?
- What threats might affect the performance of business?

Asking these basic questions for every situation will serve the EP specialist well—as long as he or she knows where to find the answers.

Information Collection and Source Management

The proper collection of information and the vetting of information providers (sources) can significantly enhance an EP program. Source management is critical to the intelligence process. Sources should be varied (human sources, Web sites, news feeds, broadcast media, etc.). All sources should be profiled, rated, and databased.

Source rating and profiling enables the EP specialist to understand the source's productivity, consistency, and reliability. An unreliable source can corrupt an intelligence regime at its very core. Source databasing makes it possible to track the reliability of the multiple sources needed. While source vetting is essential to the generation of reliable knowledge, information must be corroborated unless it is from a proven, impeccable source. The best practice is to link information gathered by multiple, individually rated sources to corroborate and verify information gathered.

Sample Source Rating Scheme

Reliability: A – F

A = Known to be a highly reliable source (e.g., the U.S. State Department)
B = Believed to be a highly reliable source
C = Respected source, no reason to doubt content validity
D = Known to have mixed credibility; should attempt to corroborate any information from this source
E = Not a reliable source; prone to sensationalism
F = Poor or highly biased information; do not use

Information Processing and Intelligence Analysis

Once reliable information has been gathered, a thorough and thoughtful analysis must be conducted. In the analytical process, the EP specialist should ask the following questions:

- Is this information important to the principal?
- What more do I need to know about it?
- What is the potential impact or outcome?
- What actions are to be taken?

The EP specialist should evaluate any piece of information against the above questions. Good intelligence differs from mere information in that it provides answers to those questions.

The following are two versions of travel security information:

- **Mere Information**

    China: Police and military officials were deployed in

Tiananmen Square on June 4, 2009, to prevent protests from occurring in commemoration of the 20th anniversary of the Tiananmen Square massacre. Despite the sensitivity of the anniversary, Tiananmen Square was opened to visitors on June 4. In Australia, protests were reported in commemoration of the 1989 student-led protest in Beijing.

- **Good Intelligence**[21]

Summary

Chinese authorities have reportedly stepped up security in Beijing to thwart any potential unrest associated with the 20th anniversary of the Tiananmen Square Massacre (June Fourth Incident) on June 4. Reports indicate that security personnel have increased patrols and been questioning and searching pedestrians on streets and in neighborhoods around the iconic Tiananmen Square. Authorities have also reportedly tightened media restrictions and been refusing to allow foreign journalists to film at the square.

Background and Analysis

On the night of June 3-4, 1989, the government ordered the People's Liberation Army to launch a major crackdown on student demonstrators who had been occupying Tiananmen Square to push for pro-democracy reforms. The death toll remains secret, although some accounts claim security personnel killed hundreds, perhaps thousands, of protesters. Many more people suffered injuries.

Major protests are unlikely, although small groups of demonstrators may attempt to engage in acts of civil

---

[21] Example courtesy of iJET Risk Systems.

disobedience similar to those witnessed during the Olympic Games. Security personnel will act quickly and decisively to quell any potential unrest. Problems are possible in Beijing, Shanghai, and other major cities, although the largest commemorative events and demonstrations are likely in Hong Kong, where large rallies have already occurred.

Advice

Stay away from Tiananmen Square through June 5; expect a heavy uniformed and plainclothes security presence in the area. Use caution around university campuses. Do not discuss politics or the 1989 events in public. Strictly avoid demonstrators. Remain cooperative and nonconfrontational if confronted by security personnel. Do not bring any media into the country that discusses the Tiananmen events or is otherwise critical of the communist regime.

One can clearly see the difference between the preceding examples. The first, while perhaps timely, is not much more than a brief summary of an event, likely based solely on a news article. The second example contains basically the same information as the first, but provides context and background, and most importantly includes insight and advice. While an EP specialist can over time cultivate the skills to conduct this type of analysis, it is typically more efficient to rely on one of the many services that provide this higher level of analysis and intelligence.

Production and Dissemination

The final step in the intelligence cycle involves the production and distribution of information in a format that is useful and digestible. Conventionally, this is conceived of as a report that is delivered to the client. The EP specialist can use the report as a tool for sparking dialogue with the principal and for planning the best ways to ensure the principal's safety.

Understanding the Threat Environment

As mentioned earlier, there are two general types of risk: intrinsic and dynamic. Intrinsic risks may take longer to understand, but they may be the easier of the two to counter. When an EP specialist goes to a site to conduct advance work or pre-trip surveys, he or she is seeking to understand the intrinsic threats. By driving the possible routes from the airport to a meeting site, the EP specialist is getting the lay of the land—looking for chokepoints, other hazards, emergency resources, and efficient routes. Similarly, when an EP specialist audits the hotel or event site, he or she should be looking for the threats that are inherent or intrinsic to that particular site. It may also be useful, and on occasion critical, to expand the research and ascertain what threats are inherent to the whole city or even the country.

On the other hand, dynamic threats, while relatively easy to conceive of, are perhaps more difficult to fully understand and reconcile with the principal's risk profile. By definition, the dynamic threat oscillates—peaks, plateaus, and troughs pervade the threat environment—often in an unpredictable or barely predictable manner.

While the intrinsic threat can be ascertained through several sources, including the U.S. State Department and even the Lonely Planet Travel Guide (www.lonelyplanet.com), understanding, analyzing, and producing intelligence regarding the dynamic threat involves a bit more expertise. At the most sophisticated levels, those responsible for providing intelligence regarding the dynamic threat environment must be schooled in behavioral psychology, history, trend analysis, and statistics.

To clarify, as a location undergoes a rapid increase in dynamic threat (perhaps due to an increasing and sustained trend in kidnapping), the local law enforcement agencies and institutions will be in a stage of adjustment and may not be able to mitigate the threat adequately. Over time, if the threat persists, the institutions and agencies may adapt and eventually overcome the threat or at least provide adequate measures against it. During this adjustment phase, it is up to the EP specialist to fill the gap.

The EP specialist who can capture and understand the dynamic threat environment (or who has access to a provider of the necessary information) is most likely to succeed at the task of protecting the principal.

Other Threat Domains

The threats most commonly considered in executive protection are those threats related to physical security, such as crime, kidnapping, and terrorism. However, to offer the highest degree of executive protection, the EP specialist should be informed about even more threat domains.

Health

Especially in international travel, health considerations are a major issue. In terms of probability, illness and injury are the factors most likely to interfere with business and the safety of the executive. Fortunately, health is the domain that is easiest to stay informed about and mitigate. Many countries' public health agencies provide free, robust, and accurate health data for travelers.

Sample Public Health Agencies

Australia
Department of Foreign Affairs and Trade
http://www.smartraveller.gov.au/zw-cgi/view/Advice/

Canada
Public Health Agency of Canada
http://www.phac-aspc.gc.ca/tmp-pmv/index-eng.php

France
Health Monitoring Institute
http://www.invs.sante.fr/

Hong Kong
Travel Health Service
http://www.travelhealth.gov.hk/textonly/eindex.html

Spain
Ministry of Health
http://www.msc.es/profesionales/saludPublica/sanidadExterior/salud/home.htm

United Kingdom
Department of Health
http://www.nhs.uk/Healthcareabroad/Pages/Healthcareabroad.aspx

National Travel Health Network and Centre
http://www.nathnac.org/

United States of America
Centers for Disease Control and Prevention (CDC)
http://wwwn.cdc.gov/Travel

U.S. Department of State
http://travel.state.gov/travel

World Health Organization
http://www.who.int/ith/en/index.html

Also, it is essential to understand any health conditions or complications the protectee might have, such as diabetes, heart disease, or asthma. If the principal has a serious condition, the EP specialist should find out where proper care for the principal can be obtained during the proposed trip.

Climate and Environment

Also worth taking into account in a robust intelligence regime is the threat posed by the climate and the environment of the destination. A visit to the Dominican Republic during hurricane season requires a different posture than a visit during the calm spring months. Similarly, unpredictable heat waves or cold snaps may affect scheduled activities and require a change of plans. Executive protection specialists can stay informed of changing climate and environmental conditions through a variety of free sources. The following are among the most trusted and best recognized:

- U.S. National Oceanic and Atmospheric Administration: www.noaawatch.gov
- The Weather Channel: www.weather.com
- Weather Underground: www.wunderground.com
- Accuweather: www.accuweather.com

Threats Regarding Personal and Professional Associations

It is also important for the EP specialist to be informed of threats to the protectee due to the protectee's professional and personal associations. Some of these are threats directed toward the principal's corporate brand by social justice networks and animal rights activists, who might lash out at the company by attacking or harassing the protectee, whom they perceive to be an "agent of injustice." The principal's relationship with the corporation is not the only association that lends itself to scrutiny, disdain, and hatred from social justice networks. The principal may also attract attention due to the boards he or she sits on, clubs to which he or she belongs, outspoken friends and associates, and even sporting activities, such as hunting or fishing. While discovering all plots against the principal is unlikely, and probably unnecessary, information can be collected, compiled, and analyzed according to the same intelligence process outlined previously. Some simple and free measures can be taken to monitor Web sites, special interest forums, on-line videos, blogs, and new sites. Google's Alert tool (www.google.com/alerts) is the most robust service of this type. The simple process for creating an alert is shown in the box below.

```
Create a Google Alert

Enter the topic you wish to monitor.

Search terms: [                    ]
Type:         [ Comprehensive ▼ ]
How often:    [ as-it-happens ▼ ]
Your email:   [                    ]

              [ Create Alert ]

Google will not sell or share your email address.
```

The Google Alert tool constantly searches the Web, looking for as many search terms as one gives it. The tool then delivers the results to the user's e-mail. If an EP specialist set the search term to be the principal's name, such as "Rudolph Giuliani"[22] for example, Google will crawl the Internet looking for new mentions of Mayor Giuliani's name as they are posted. For a client with a very high profile (like Rudolph Giuliani), the EP specialist may want to focus the Google Alert tool to search

---

[22] A search term likely to be more comprehensive might actually look like this: "Rudy OR Rudolph * Giuliani" OR "Mayor Giuliani." For advanced search techniques, see http://www.googleguide.com/advanced_operators_reference.html.

only blogs or special interest group forums. Otherwise, the name may come up in too many irrelevant citations to be useful in the security effort.

"Self-Inflicted" Threats

Another threat domain consists of threats inflicted or imposed on the principal by his or her own actions. To study this domain requires understanding the principal's behavior. Of particular interest are habits of alcohol use or overindulgence; schedules or routines that are regular or predictable; ill-considered disclosure of personal information on social networking media sites like Facebook and Twitter; and activities or hobbies with inherent threats (open ocean yachting, aviation, skydiving, etc.). Understanding the threats that the principal subjects himself or herself to gives the EP specialist an opportunity to develop countermeasures to lower the protectee's risk profile.

Does Intelligence Really Make a Difference?

During the late summer and early fall of 1975, the Irish Republican Army dramatically escalated its frightful campaign to drive British forces from Northern Ireland. Terrorist cells struck commercial, military, and law enforcement targets across England 17 times between August and November, killing or wounding scores of people in pubs, restaurants, hotels, and private homes. In those days, before the advent of travel intelligence, the evening news remained the primary provider of useful information for the private citizen. That citizen would hear how, in the British capital, a blast took place at the National Westminster Bank on High Street, a bombing at the Hilton Hotel on Park Lane killed two people and injured 63 others, letter bombs were sent to residents of Notting Hill in mid-

September, a deadly bombing occurred at the Ritz Hotel in Piccadilly on October 8, a huge bomb containing 27.5 lb. of gelignite was discovered and defused at Lockett's Restaurant on Marsham Street, the bombing of Trattoria Fiori on Mount Street in cosmopolitan Mayfair injured 17 people (including two Americans) on October 30, and the bombing of Scotts Restaurant—also in Mayfair—killed one person and wounded 15 other patrons.

The list of attacks and attempted attacks against property or people associated with the British government generally, the military, or the police, and against innocent bystanders, went on and on until the terrorist cell responsible for that brutal period was discovered and thwarted. The events received prominent coverage in the United Kingdom, but in the United States many of these attacks were not reported, so there was no real sense that there was a clear and present danger for those contemplating travel to the British capital. The Americans injured in the Trattoria Fiori attack proved to have had only a vague notion that there was an IRA problem at the time of their visit; they were ill-equipped to face the security challenges at a critical time. The lack of information, of intelligence, could have cost them their lives.

While the days of IRA bombings largely faded into history with the signing of the Good Friday Agreement in 1998, a new security challenge revealed itself on the morning of July 7, 2005. The incident began innocently enough, with reports that a blast of unknown origin had shut down Tube services in central London. Most believed there had been an industrial accident, and despite some reported injuries and the aforementioned history of terrorist attacks, few Londoners expected much more than to be late for work that day. Just days before, on July 2, a tunnel collapse at Gerrards Cross had led to major delays between Marylebone Station and Birmingham, and buses had been enlisted to ferry travelers during the ensuing repair work.

Among the many international travelers visiting the British capital that morning, those who were being tracked by leading intelligence firms providers received alerts that warned of potential disruptions within minutes of the first reports of trouble.

While Londoners looked for other ways to get to work, intelligence firm clients were given a range of options to navigate a city gradually awakening to chaos.

While Londoners looked for other ways to get to work, intelligence firm clients were given a range of options to navigate a city gradually awakening to chaos. They were directed to online maps, given the latest updates put out by London Transport authorities, and apprised of related road disruptions via cell phone, Blackberry, or Internet. This gift of sight amid a population struggling to see the emerging crisis would be tested throughout the day. As reports emerged that a double-decker bus had exploded in Russell Square and that multiple devices had detonated at various Underground stations, all hope that the morning commute had been thrown into disorder by an industrial mishap were erased and city authorities moved quickly to cordon off affected areas.

What did intelligence firm clients learn? For example, clients of iJET Intelligent Risk Systems received the following critical update, whose title had changed from "Major Incident Halts Tube Services" to "Terrorist Attacks Update 3":

> A series of explosions hit London beginning at approximately 0850 local time July 7, shutting down central Underground and bus services. British officials have con-

firmed that the incidents were a coordinated series of terrorist attacks. An updated casualty figure from officials in
London at 1430 local time states at least 45 people were
killed and 1,000 injured; those numbers will likely go up.
All of the explosions occurred within a two-hour time
frame between 0851 and 0947 local time. The incidents
have led to major chaos in London; much of central London is closed off to vehicles, and gridlock is hampering
transportation in other areas. Limit movements within
London.

Officials said public transport would likely be closed for
the duration of July 7. Some commuter train services into
and out of London may resume operations by late after-
noon or early evening. Victoria and Liverpool Street stations are also expected to reopen soon, but a police spo-
kesperson said that it is "extremely unlikely" Tube service
will resume July 7.

The Gatwick Express is reportedly operating reduced service; Heathrow Express and Stansted Express services are
experiencing disruptions.

Heathrow Airport (LHR) officials have confirmed that
flights are operating as scheduled. Travelers to London
airports should seek alternate methods of transportation,
including taxis, if rail services are not operating. British officials have advised travelers arriving at London airports to
avoid traveling into the city for the time being if possible.
If at a hotel in the London area, do not check out until you
have confirmed the availability of your transportation.

The explosions on the Tube occurred at the following locations and times:

- Between Aldgate East and Liverpool Street tube stations
  (City of London) at 0851;

- Between Russell Square and King's Cross tube stations
  (Central London) at 0856;

- At Edgware Rd tube station (NW London) at 0917;

- An explosion also occurred on Bus 30 at Woburn Place, a street running between Russell Square and Tavistock Place (City of London) at 0947.

Hospitals are refusing non-emergency cases. A number of businesses have shut down in central London.

Both mobile phone service and land-line service have been affected by the large number of users trying to make calls. Service may be unavailable. Text messaging on mobile phone networks is typically more reliable than voice communication when networks are overloaded.

Telephone numbers for additional information:

- Police and Casualty Emergency Hotline: 0870-1566-344;

- Information Line: 0870-333-1330 (in London; provides information on incidents).

For updated information about transportation in the London area, visit the Transport for London Web site at www.tfl.gov.uk

Very quickly, customers were advised about current conditions across the spectrum of the transportation sector, as iJET anticipated the aftereffects of the Tube shutdown. iJET's health team, meanwhile, had begun to determine the hazards associated with the event and issued the following alert in tandem with the company's security advisories:

Health authorities in London are telling persons who suffered an injury that penetrated the skin during the July 7 bombings to receive prophylactic treatment to prevent hepatitis B. The treatment consists of a series of hepatitis B vaccinations that should begin as soon as possible before July 14. The vaccine series is given in four doses at 0, 1, 2 and 12 months. Hepatitis B hyperimmune globulin (HBIG) given at the start of the vaccine series may improve efficacy of the series.

Other people at risk for blood-borne diseases as a result of the explosions include people who sustained injuries as a result of providing assistance to victims, and those with superficial exposures of skin or mucous membranes to blood of victims. Although at lesser risk, these people should also receive post-exposure prophylaxis for hepatitis B.

Doctors are also recommending that blood specimens be drawn now, in three months and in six months and tested for hepatitis B and C. A group of British infectious disease experts considered the risk of HIV due to the explosions to be so low as not to require action (though counseling and testing could be provided as needed).

Experts have identified no evidence that the smoke associated with the bombings contained unusual chemicals. Health authorities say the risk of developing long-term effects from a one-time exposure is very small, especially if the individual had no significant acute respiratory symptoms at the time of the explosion.

People who suffered severe eye irritation or respiratory effects due to smoke inhalation at the time of the bombings should receive a follow-up evaluation by their physician.

Psychological reactions to the bombings are common, but generally resolve with time. Seek treatment for persistent symptoms.

For days after the July 7 attacks, clients received alerts about disruptions to the transportation system, as Tube and bus services came slowly back and airports cleared flight backlogs caused by heightened security measures.

For EP providers, navigating London in lockdown mode required granular information to minimize exposure during point-to-point travel. Above and beyond the attacks themselves, planned or spontaneous vigils by a grieving population snarled streets across central London. On July 14, clients received a warning that a mass vigil would tie up travel near Trafalgar Square, while on July 18 an alert summarized the slow return to normalcy on London's Tube:

> Much of London's public transportation services are operating as scheduled July 18, with the exception of some limited services on certain London Underground lines:
>
> - Circle Line: Services remain suspended.
>
> - Hammersmith and City: There are no services between Paddington and Barking; services are operating only between Hammersmith and Paddington.
>
> - Metropolitan Line: There are no services between Moorgate and Aldgate.
>
> - Piccadilly Line: There are no services between Hyde Park Corner and Arnos Grove and between Rayners Lane and Uxbridge.
>
> Replacement bus services are operating between stations that are not being serviced. Bus service has largely resumed normal schedules, but service in the following areas may be subject to detours: Aldgate, King's Cross and Russell Square.
>
> Investigations into the July 7 incidents are continuing; expect lingering delays in the areas where authorities are still conducting investigations. All roads have been reopened except in the immediate vicinity of the above locations, where security cordons remain.
>
> Bomb threats are common after major terrorist attacks, regardless of location. Repeated hoaxes could tax emergency response capabilities and create considerable disruptions if they force the evacuation of trains or public places.
>
> Resources for additional information:
>
> - Police and Casualty Emergency Hotline: 0870-156-6344;
>
> - Transport for London Web site: www.tfl.gov.uk (for updated information about transportation around London);

- Information Line: 0870-333-1330 (in London, provides information on incidents).

That return to normalcy was shattered on July 21. iJET clients were alerted to the fact that yet another attack appeared to be underway on London's transport network. The company's second update conveyed the following information:

UPDATE 2 to July 21 alert:

London police officials have reported that the July 21 incidents on London's Underground (Tube) and bus system involved four "near simultaneous" explosions, but the bombs or detonators used were apparently of a lower level than those used in the July 7 attacks. Police have also cordoned off University College Hospital in Bloomsbury near Warren Street Station, where they are reportedly searching for a suspect connected to the incidents. One casualty was reported at the Warren Street Station. An explosion was reported on the number 26 bus near Hackney and Colombia Roads in east London's Bethnal Green. Emergency crews are at the scenes.

The blasts led to the evacuation of the Shepherd's Bush, Oval and Warren Street Tube stations. Officials also confirmed a Code Amber alert and shut down additional tube services. As of 1540, services on the Bakerloo, Piccadilly, Victoria, Northern and Hammersmith and City lines have been suspended; further closures of services on other Tube lines are possible. Media sources have stated that dummy explosions using detonators may have sparked the evacuation of the tube stations; police have confirmed there are no reports that chemical agents were used. Security has been heightened, and security forces have cordoned off streets in the vicinity of the tube stations.

There have been no reports of impact to airport or flight services. Mobile services and regular phone lines around London may be disrupted. Authorities are urging individuals to make only urgent, brief calls to prevent the phone networks from overloading.

Emergency services were called to the tube stations shortly before 1230 local time, but delays along the affected tube services could continue for up to 48 hours. Monitor local media for latest updates. Emergency contact: 999.

Some of the major road closures:

- Hampstead Road junction with Euston Road, Tottenham Court Road and Great Russell Street. Uxbridge Road is closed in the Notting Hill - Shepherds Bush area.

- A10 Both Ways Shoreditch, Shoreditch High Street Junction With Old Street (A5201)

- A202 Both Ways Lambeth, Camberwell New Road/Harleyford Street Junction With Clapham Road / Kenington Park Road .

- A400 Both Ways Soho, Tottenham Court Road Junction With Warren Street (Warren Street Underground Station)

Use other modes of transport. Contact London Underground regarding the current status for your travel plans.

London Underground Unlimited (for subway service information, including real-time service updates): Phone: 020-7918-4040; available online at www.tfl.gov.uk/tfl/

For days thereafter, London and other British cities were disrupted by false alarms and security operations. Travelers equipped with information offered by iJET and other providers were able to navigate the chaos, rather than being glued to television news reports as in 1975.

Intelligence alone could not have saved the lives of those killed in the blasts in 1975 or 2005, but the technological leaps in the decades since the IRA savaged London have made available a level of "ground truth" that could have helped potential victims avoid areas being targeted by terrorist movements, such as London's Mayfair neighborhood in the mid-'70s. Again, those on London's Tube, or that bus in Russell's Square, would not have been spared death by having access to private intelligence that day, but the effects of a terrorist strike in a major city have broad implications far beyond the point of attack.

For EP providers, the inability to move with certainty and according to rehearsed scenarios through a major metropolitan area could spell disaster. The unknown is a dangerous enemy, and being caught in stopped traffic for an undetermined period with no egress is a nightmare. One of the primary rules of successful EP is varying routes to keep potential adversaries guessing where the principal is headed. It is thus critical to know when one or more of those routes have been compromised. The successful EP provider well knows that it is important to identify as many routes as possible, minimize potential choke-points, and maximize safe havens. In

> **Actionable intelligence could make the difference between success and failure, or life and death.**

an unfolding situation like that which took place in London on July 7, all bets are off unless the EP specialist is armed with the encyclopedic knowledge of a local cab driver. Actionable intelligence is a critical component in successfully confronting the unknown and could make the difference between success and failure, or life and death.

Planning alternative routes on the ground is a must. Air travel, however, poses unique problems for EP providers, particularly when using commercial airlines. In early August 2006, alerts dispatched by private intelligence firms informed clients that all UK airports were placed on critical alert following the discovery of an alleged plot to bomb U.S.-bound flights. While television and Internet sources reported the events with few details and conflicting advice for travelers, intelligence providers were able to leverage contacts in the airline industry and law enforcement to gain critical details regarding impediments to travel and increasingly tight security measures (such as secondary searches at boarding gates) for those able to travel at all. The implications for business travelers were severe, as laptops and other proprietary items held by those already in transit were suddenly banned as carry-ons. Intelligence providers were able to offer advice on how to secure vital information before leaving equipment behind or checking it for storage.

For those awaiting word prior to attempting to reach an airport in the UK, intelligence providers went so far as to describe the scene at check-in counters and to estimate how long it might take to be processed. For EP specialists, this ground truth is a critical component in determining whether the principal can travel, or if he or she should shelter in place until the situation has returned to some semblance of normalcy. Hours and days lost to indecision can be costly.

Clients of iJET received the following alert update (the fourth of many as the crisis unfolded):

> Disruptions continue Aug. 13, particularly at London Heathrow (LHR) and Stansted (STN) airports, due to heightened security procedures for flights from and within the United Kingdom in the wake of an alleged plot to bring down U.S.-bound aircraft originating in the U.K. Contact your travel providers for status on all flights as a precaution.

> The British Airports Authority is tracking average delay times at selected U.K. airports at: www.baa.co.uk.

> London Airport Disruptions

> London Heathrow Airport (LHR): One-third of all flights

originating at LHR will be canceled Aug. 13 due to heightened security measures. Confirm flights before leaving for the airport.

London Gatwick Airport (LGW): Some flight delays and cancellations continue at LGW. Confirm flights.

London Stansted Airport (STN): Ryanair (FR) and British Airways (BA) have canceled roughly 20 percent of their flights at STN Aug. 13 (approximately 60 flights combined). Confirm flights before leaving for the airport.

All U.K. airports were placed on critical alert Aug. 10 and the overall terror alert for the country was raised to "critical" as a precaution. Before requesting flight cancellations, authorities imposed strict rules regarding carry-on luggage. All passengers are required to check hand luggage on outbound flights. Officials continue to impose the following restrictions as airports resume normal operations:

- Authorities are only permitting passengers to carry passports and other essentials such as wallets, small purses and keys (but not electrical key fobs) after they pass inspection and put them in airport-issued, clear plastic bags. All other materials must go in checked luggage. Laptops may not be carried onto flights. Individuals and companies must determine the best course of action in order to safeguard vital information.

- Liquids and gels, potable or otherwise, are prohibited aboard aircraft. Medications and baby formula are permitted, but expect extra scrutiny if traveling with these items. Passengers will need to verify medications as authentic, and screeners will likely check if the name listed on the prescription is the same as on the ticket.

- All passengers boarding U.S.-bound flights will undergo secondary searches at boarding gates for the foreseeable future.

British police arrested 24 people Aug. 10 in connection

with a plot to blow up several airliners traveling from the U.K. to the U.S. Officials believe the suspects, who were reportedly planning to stage a "practice run" in the coming days, planned to smuggle liquid explosives aboard in their carry-on luggage. On Aug. 11, officials froze bank accounts belonging to the suspects, all of whom were British citizens of Pakistani heritage. Details regarding the plot, sometimes contradictory, continue to emerge.

By the time the company's last alert on the crisis was issued on August 20, fully 10 days after the incident began, flights had mostly resumed, but the rules and regulations were still being formed and reformed by authorities. It is this kind of full-spectrum, around-the-clock support that makes it possible for an EP provider to successfully serve his or her principal.

Intelligence Resources

Many intelligence sources and subscription products are available to support EP specialists, and no source is all-sufficient. However, some firms can provide EP specialists with a solid foundation on which to build a comprehensive intelligence capability.

One of the best sources of country and city intelligence with 24/7 monitoring is provided by iJET International, Inc. (www.ijet.com), through its Worldcue® Global Control Center. The author favors this service for several reasons. First, it is fairly comprehensive, covering over 400 locations and information across 10 domains. These domains cover security, health, transportation, entry/exit, weather/environment, financial, communications, legal, culture, and language. But more important, they provide global alert coverage 24/7. While most providers summarize the news and mainly provide after-the-fact reporting, iJET gives predictive alerts to give the client advance notice on strikes, major demonstrations, impending civil unrest, and more.

Worldcue subscribers can set up locations of interest and have any new alerts forwarded to their e-mail address or cell phone. A few weeks before a trip, the EP specialist should turn the feature on to get a sense of what is happening in the locations the principal will be visiting. Then, once the EP specialist or principal is en route, the system will keep the client apprised of any issues that are brewing or major events that may affect the principal's plans. As part of the service, a client with a question can call into iJET's 24x7 Watch Center and speak directly with an analyst.

Operations center at iJET Intelligent Risk Systems, Annapolis, Maryland.

Generally, an EP specialist will want to augment this baseline information with additional information, depending on the parameters of the trip. The following are some recommended sites:

- **General Aviation and Global Flight Information**
    — **www.airnav.com:** Run by AirNav, LLC, in At-

lanta, Georgia, this site provides detailed information on airports, including runway information, maps, ownership, fuel services, and much more.

— **www.flightstats.com:** This site is run by Conductive Technology Corp. in Portland, Oregon. It provides real-time flight information, as well as details on flight schedules, on-time performance, and many other types of airport, airline, and flight data. In addition, a user can sign up to get alerts when a flight is delayed, takes off, or is about to land.

- **Embassy Information**

— **www.embassyworld.com:** This long-lived site provides a searchable database of embassy and consulate locations for almost any nation state. Most entries have a link to the embassy Web site.

— **www.osac.gov:** Run in cooperation with the U.S. State Department, the Overseas Security Advisory Council (OSAC) is an excellent resource and provides access to the State Department's regional security officers (RSOs) stationed around the world.

The tale from the field at the beginning of this chapter presented an after-the-fact summary of the July 7, 2005, bombings in London. That news-style summary condensed the day's terrible events into a few short sentences. However, that orderly, calm presentation is not what ordinary Londoners received when word of the attacks began to spread. As might be expected, they received details bit by bit and could only hope to piece together the story and make prudent decisions about staying or going. By contrast, among the international travelers in London, those who were clients of private intelligence firms benefited from having teams of analysts work around the clock to collect and analyze information from many sources, then process, produce, and disseminate the most useful and reliable information. Without having to spend time digging for that data themselves, they or their EP specialists received valuable information designed to help them make the best decisions.

5.
Protecting the Reluctant Principal

Tale from the Field

The chief executive officer of a major financial institution in the Midwest needed protection but simply did not want it.

Why did he need it? He held a high-profile position in an organization of national significance. His name and picture appeared often in the media, and for various reasons his firm and its industry were widely unpopular. The city in which he worked suffered from an extremely high rate of violent crime. Nationwide, many executives in positions similar to his received various levels of EP service. There was a history of attacks against persons in positions like his, and he had been threatened, seriously, more than once by disgruntled business partners and former employees. Security at his home was suspect because he had just fired his house manager, who turned out to have a criminal record and was well aware of the home's expensive contents and the workings of its security systems.

Why did the executive not want protection? The executive enjoyed driving himself to work, clearly knew the city well, and considered himself a tough character who was savvy about dealing with danger. He did not want to be seen as afraid or to be hindered in his movements. Also, he was unwilling to put up with what he considered the inconvenience of EP simply to avoid the low-likelihood (but high-consequence) eventuality of an attack against him personally.

The preceding tale from the field represents a genuine, widespread problem. In performing risk assessments and security planning for leading corporations around the United States and abroad, the author has interviewed many top executives face-to-face. They often say they know they face some risks and should be protected, and they understand why their company needs to have them protected. However, some of them still object to receiving EP. They may think it will be inconvenient; they may not like the idea of having EP specialists around them; they may feel EP will make them look weak; or they may have some other objection to receiving the protective services they admit they need.

This is all perfectly understandable. The problem is that these executives are typically the most valuable human assets their organizations have. An attack on an executive hurts the company. An executive who is injured or killed cannot do the company's work. Moreover, an attack on an executive upsets other employees, requires an immediate shift in the chain of command, and makes the company look incompetent—as if it cannot protect its assets.

There is clearly a conflict in situations like this: the company legitimately needs to protect the executive, but the executive does not want the protection. It is a challenge unlike others in security—because other corporate assets do not speak up to say whether they want to be protected. Proprietary information does not complain when security personnel encrypt it. Aircraft do not object when they are locked securely in a hangar. But the top executive may not be shy about saying he or she does not care for executive protection. Still, if the company has a security

> **For protecting a reluctant principal, this chapter details EP solutions that are currently working in corporate America.**

director or EP manager, that person may well be held responsible if the executive is harmed—even if the executive rejected the protection that was offered. So how can one protect an executive who does not want to receive protection?

For the challenge of protecting the reluctant principal, this chapter proposes several solutions. These are EP approaches that are currently working effectively in corporate America. The approaches may not always be an EP specialist's first choice. (First choice might be to surround the principal 24/7 and move into his or her guest room at home.) However, the solutions provided here are practical ways to serve a reluctant principal. This chapter proposes a low-profile approach to close-in protection, describing two different methods. It also describes a cluster of EP techniques that are particularly useful when attempting to protect a reluctant principal.

When protecting any principal, and especially when protecting a reluctant principal, an EP manager should take the following managerial steps, no matter what EP approach is being applied:

- Understand the basic principles of executive protection and execute them flawlessly.
- Be purposeful in the EP program and understand the interaction of elements within the protective system.
- Follow the "understand–plan–execute" strategy as shown in the graphic below:

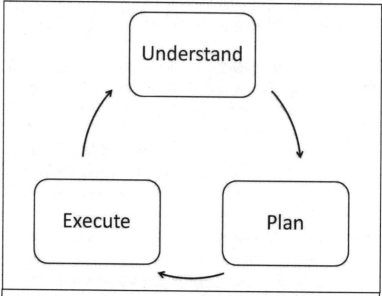

No matter what approach one takes to executive protection—highly visible or behind the scenes—or how amenable the principal is to protection, the cycle of understanding, planning, and executing drives the EP program and keeps it on the right path.

Low-Profile, Close-in Protection

To provide unobtrusive, in-person protection to a principal, the EP specialist can experiment with a couple of different methods, which this book calls "the name game" and "there but not there."

The Name Game

In this approach, the EP program places a trained EP specialist in close proximity to the principal, but—to anyone who asks—he is introduced as an executive-level assistant. The particular title chosen should be one that is plausible within the company. It could be executive assistant, assistant chief of staff, special assistant to the president, or any other appropriate title. This person should be primarily a protection specialist. Secondarily, the person should know how to do the job that the title reflects. The person will genuinely fulfill both roles, but the more important role is his EP duty.

This person will need business cards showing his officially recognized title in the company. He will be introduced as the special assistant and will look and act the part—as far as everyone else can tell. He will accompany the principal to outside meetings, on travel, and in other cases where the risk assessment suggests that in-person protection is needed. He will stay in close proximity. Assigning the person to two roles (assistant and EP specialist) may help overcome the reluctant principal's objections. Certainly, having a special assistant should not make an executive look weak or feel cramped.

There But Not There

A second technique is to be there but not there. When the EP program determines that the risk level of an event warrants in-person protection, the EP manager or chief security officer informs the principal of the risk and says that protection will be provided—that is, an EP specialist will be at the site, as near as practical to the principal. However, the two parties—EP specialist and principal—will not arrive together, will not stand together, and will not appear to be together. In fact, in some cases, the principal may not even know which person in the area is his EP specialist. Nevertheless, a protector will be there.

This approach becomes possible by balancing two factors: proximity and countersurveillance. Most attackers attack from a very close distance. Therefore, it is best for the EP specialist to be close to the principal in order to intervene. The EP specialist needs both the judgment to know when to back off and the wherewithal to be effective. This skill set is developed through training and experience. In any case, it is ineffective to be very far away. If the EP specialist is no more than 20 or 25 feet away, he may still be able to intervene in an attack.

Another major benefit that a trained and experience EP specialist brings to the protective game is the ability to telegraph his presence to those who may pose a threat. The would-be attacker will identify and relate to that presence. The author knows from experience and documented close-in attacks that the adversary often redirects his focus and goes after a softer target. A report on the Exceptional Case Study Project conducted by the U.S. Secret Service notes:[23]

> Consistent with their motives, many…attackers and would-be attackers considered more than one target before moving to attack. For example, several individuals whose primary motive was notoriety considered attacking public officials like Governors and Members of Congress before ultimately deciding to attack the President or Vice President; they calculated that an attack on the President or Vice President would receive more attention. Assailants often made final decisions about whom to attack because an opportunity for attack pre-

---

[23] Robert Fein and Bryan Vossekuil, *Protective Intelligence and Threat Assessment Investigations* (Washington, DC: US Department of Justice, 2000), p. 20.

sented itself or because they perceived another target was unapproachable.

Closer is usually better, but sometimes the EP specialist can create an advantage by using his distance to perform counter-surveillance. In other words, the EP specialist might prefer to be close, but if he must be farther away, he can at least put himself in a good position to watch the scene surrounding the principal. By watching the scene carefully, he may observe tell-tale signs of an attacker: possible weapons concealed under clothing, nervous behavior, clothing that is inappropriate for the weather or the event, etc. (The application of countersurveillance to close-in protection is discussed in greater detail in Chapter 6, The Attack Vector.)

Both of these approaches to serving the reluctant principal—"the name game" and "there but not there"—can help an EP specialist protect a key corporate asset, even if that asset would prefer not to be protected. It is worth noting, too, that both of these approaches may benefit from variety in the EP work force. EP specialists of varying appearances may be able to blend into the scene better than a person who looks like the majority of EP specialists. Likewise, EP specialists of varying backgrounds and experience may have different work styles that allow them to fit into different settings without attracting attention.

Other Techniques

The following are several techniques that can be used to safeguard the reluctant principal in ways other than close-in protection:

- Security umbrella

- Behind-the-scenes risk reduction
- Key-point protection
- Preparation to do more
- Leverage

Security Umbrella

The image of a security umbrella is meant to suggest a protective apparatus that comfortably accompanies the protectee at a decent distance. Placing the reluctant principal under a 24/7 security umbrella means making his safety the responsibility of the EP program at all times, around the clock. However, the protection program does not assign an EP specialist to accompany him at all times. Instead, the program keeps its distance and directs a watchful eye over issues that affect the principal's safety, moving in close only when needed (and allowed).

The EP program consistently monitors risks to the principal, staying aware of his activities, providing secure local transportation for commuting and other activities as appropriate, arranging security for his out-of-town travel, serving as a resource for his home security, ensuring the

> **Security umbrella: a protective apparatus that comfortably accompanies the protectee, decently distant.**

security of his office space, and providing other research, liaison, and services as appropriate. If the principal plans to travel outside his home country, the EP manager should develop a crisis plan to activate security support if something goes wrong abroad. Doing this homework ahead of time shows a level of commitment to protect the executive even if no EP specialist goes along on the trip. (Chapter 8, Emergency Extraction of the Principal, addresses this concept in greater detail.) In addition, covering the principal's family with the security umbrella gives added credibility to the EP program, supports the mission in general, and helps the principal feel comfortable about the family's safety when he is traveling out of town.

If the risk level allows for this more distant approach to EP, then it should be continued for the sake of the reluctant principal. However, if the risk level should rise suddenly, the security apparatus may have to move in a little closer. (This book's appendix contains a customizable matrix designed to aid in quickly rolling out new security practices to match shifting risk levels.) If the principal declines the offer of more closely provided security (such as daily driving service or in-person accompaniment to events), the EP manager should make the case for more protection, but ultimately it is the principal's decision. However, those decisions should be based on fact, not guesswork.

> **This book's appendix contains a customizable matrix for quickly rolling out new security practices to match shifting risk levels.**

In fact, the principal's ability to accept or decline close-in protection is one more reason to know how to provide EP service from a distance. Sometimes that is all one is allowed to do.

Behind-the-Scenes Risk Reduction

Another way to serve a reluctant principal is to work behind the scenes to reduce or counteract risk factors that affect the principal. There are many steps that an EP manager can take on behalf of the principal's safety without overly intruding into or encumbering the principal's life. The EP program can take such steps as the following:

- Develop liaison with law enforcement so that if the EP program identifies a potential threat, the EP manager will know who to call and what action can be taken. Why not inform law enforcement or other authorities in advance instead of waiting for a dangerous person to show up at the principal's home or office?

- Maintain a threat file. Every potentially threatening contact (letters, phone calls, visits) should be documented and investigated fully to determine whether it is credible.

- Ensure that the principal's home security system is maintained regularly. The EP program can serve as liaison to the selected maintenance or monitoring company, taking that responsibility off the family's back and also ensuring that the system is in good order.

- Monitor crime statistics covering the principal's neighborhood. In many locations crime information is available on-line, often plotted on maps so the viewer can see the geographic concentration or dispersal of incidents. A significant rise in local crime might give the EP program cause to suggest a change of security measures. If crime does not rise significantly, the EP program can maintain current security practices in the knowledge that they are still appropriate to the risk level.

The author, who has run a long-term protective detail at a residence on the outskirts of Washington, DC, began to track home invasions that were taking place in the District of Columbia and in Montgomery and Prince George's counties in Maryland. In one home invasion, the homeowner was killed and the home was burglarized. In another home invasion, the victim was tied up but not otherwise injured while the home was burglarized. These crimes were occurring closer and closer to the protectee's home, so we contacted local law enforcement. They were able to tell us various details that we could use in devising an effective protection strategy. For example, they gave us specific crime locations, descriptions of the criminals, times of the events, etc. By not guessing but using actual crime information, we were able to keep the protective detail switched on and alert to the likely sources of danger. Law enforcement representatives believed the guilty parties were landscapers or others who had gone to the houses in advance to plan their home invasions.

- Conduct a training session with household staff and nannies to teach them to keep doors locked, not to discuss confidential information, and to become a partner with the security team so if they feel there is a problem, they know whom to contact.

- Conduct careful background screening of household staff, and refresh or update the information annually. Not everything in a person's past is readily discoverable by private-sector employers, but much information is available, and the EP program can increase the principal's security by flagging serious issues in a household employee's credit, driving, or criminal history.

This last service can bring surprising value to the principal. The tale from the field that opened this chapter mentioned a CEO who fired his house manager. The house manager later made threats against the CEO. What happened next is an example of behind-the-scenes risk reduction—but it came a little late. Because of the threat, the EP program conducted a background investigation of the fired house manager. The investigation found he was a former convict and known fraudster. The CEO's family felt vulnerable having him as an enemy, as he knew many details of the family's home, habits, and possessions, as well as the security measures employed at the house.

If the background investigation had been conducted before the house manager was hired, the principal's family might not have found itself in that predicament. Background investigation of household staff is a protective service that the EP program can readily provide to a reluctant principal. Also, if the EP program establishes liaison with the principal's spouse and family and offers to perform a security assessment of the residence, the principal will see that the EP operation is concerned about him even when he is not on the corporate clock.

Key-Point Protection

If a principal is reluctant to be accompanied to public functions or to be driven to and from work, the EP program can still provide some level of protection by concentrating its efforts on key points in the principal's movements. For example, historically most attacks against executives who were commuting to work have happened very near the house or very near the office. Fewer attacks have taken place along the commuting route, as cars tend to be moving faster and good security drivers vary their routes.

Key-point protection focuses a limited EP presence on the riskiest locations and activities.

Thus, the EP program can place a vehicle patrol near the principal's driveway (or perhaps at a moderate distance to facilitate countersurveillance) and also provide security at the point where the principal parks and enters the building. In that fashion, the EP program provides solid protection at the theoretically riskiest parts of the journey, and the principal can feel mostly or totally independent.

One client company applied the concept of key-point protection to the path from the principal's parking space in the garage to his office on the 42nd floor of a high-rise building. The risk assessment had determined that the principal faced his greatest risk in the public parking garage and along the route to his office, because it was along that path that people knew where to find him. Because the principal strongly preferred a minimalist approach to security, the EP manager set up a customized routine.

In the morning, the EP manager would be present upon the principal's arrival in the garage and escort him through various semipublic spaces until they reached the principal's office. The EP manager maintained a small office nearby so he could be on hand for emergencies or for the occasional outing on which the principal was willing to be accompanied. During the day, while the principal worked in his own office or migrated throughout the company's office space on several floors, the EP manager did not follow him around, judging that the company space was relatively secure. Instead, from his office he would engage in security planning and research, and he could watch for potential dangers by viewing CCTV images of the principal's office area and the entrances to the floor. At the end of the day, he would escort the principal to his car in the garage. At other times of the day, when the principal would leave the office to drive to meetings and activities around the city, the EP program generally did not accompany him, protect his route, or meet him at his destinations. This approach is an example of key-point protection—focusing the limited amount of EP presence that is allowed on the riskiest locations and activities. Of course, a greater security presence would be needed if the principal was attending a public event with a significant risk level.

Preparing to Do More

A business dictum states that an upward-striving employee should dress for the job he or she would like to have next. Similarly, if an EP program has a reluctant principal and is not able to provide the full level of service that the risk assessment calls for, it makes sense to prepare the program to provide that higher level of security as soon as the principal is willing to accept it. Like the ambitious employee, the EP program will appear to be (and will actually be) ready to step up its protective activities. The more able and professional the EP program can make itself, the more acceptable the principal may find the concept of closer protection.

To prepare the EP program for the next level of performance, the EP manager should encourage or require the following:

- Continuing education of EP personnel (through, for example, support for obtaining undergraduate or graduate degrees or the Certified Protection Professional (CPP) designation from ASIS International)
- Ongoing training (from in-house and outside providers)
- Regular exercises on the choreography of moving the principal
- Role play regarding adversarial interventions

If the risk level rises and the principal agrees to accept more protection, the EP manager will be able to call on trained, educated in-house personnel who understand the nuances of executive protection. Using outside contractors to protect the principal is awkward, is not recommended, and may depict the EP manager as lacking expertise and the willingness to protect the leading asset of the company. If the company's chief security officer brings in security contractors to assist in a particularly high-risk period, the EP manager should be sure to lead, not follow, them. They are unlikely to understand the corporate culture. Taking the lead will add credibility to the EP program for the future.

More details about EP training content are given in Chapter 9, Human Factor: Training and Partnerships.

Leverage

One final technique for safeguarding a reluctant principal is to maximize the number of people or agencies contributing to his or her safety, either actively or passively. If the principal is reluctant to accept full-scale coverage, it is likely that the EP program is not going to be funded at a high level. In that case, it must make the most of appropriate resources, leveraging its connections and relationships to multiply its protective service to the principal.

Such leverage might work as follows:

- Use relationships with federal, state, and local law enforcement agencies to obtain information about risks at locations where EP personnel will not be present to protect the principal. Ask local police in a city the principal plans to visit whether they are aware of upcoming protests that might affect the principal or whether they might be available (free or for pay) to patrol the area where the principal will be active.

- Use connections with the U.S. State Department (such as membership in its Overseas Security Advisory Committee) to collect risk and resource information about destinations on the principal's itinerary. Contact the regional security officers at U.S. embassies closest to the principal's destinations and ask about local risks and means of getting help for the principal if needed.

- Tap the EP manager's network of similarly situated professionals and offer to share information, advice, and even some on-the-ground services when one EP manager's principal is visiting another EP manager's city.

In sum, there are many ways to protect a principal who is reluctant to accept obvious protection measures. Some approaches involve completely behind-the-scenes efforts, others involve assigning EP specialists to be present but barely noticeable, and still others involve quietly preparing to provide protection at the next higher level if the risk so demands and the principal will accept the increased protection.

To return to this chapter's initial tale from the field, the CEO who did not want to receive protection began to change his mind once the author's firm presented a detailed risk assessment showing the dangers that faced him and his family. The risk assessment report also suggested protective measures that could be introduced gradually and that would not excessively intrude into his life. The CEO decided he was willing to shift the paradigm, realizing he would not be put in a bubble and could experience a step-by-step increase in EP services until the right level of protection was provided.

6.
The Attack Vector

The CEO of one of the largest manufacturing companies in the United States stood on stage at an international trade show. It was his moment in the spotlight, his time to announce a major new product. Cameras were rolling; reporters crowded forward. Members of his EP detail had positioned themselves wisely. Two stood near the stage, and another took a location farther out in the crowd where he could survey the scene, watching for anything suspicious. The EP team was, in theory, ready.

The way the EP specialists were positioned around the room, they had the best chance to intercept any adversary who might approach the principal from the left, from the right, or from the audience. Moreover, their positioning—some of them close, one farther out—increased the likelihood of stopping any adversary at a point farther rather than closer to the principal.

As the CEO addressed the audience, all seemed well. Then, as is often the case in EP, the unexpected struck. Two men in suits, wearing press credentials, worked their way through the crowd, climbed the short rise of steps to the stage level on the left side, and stood to the side of the stage, about 15 feet from the principal. Suddenly they strode to the center of the stage, interrupted the principal's speech, and presented him with a poster-sized pledge that they wanted the CEO to sign. It was a rather extreme environmental pledge, and they had come to embarrass the CEO into signing it or pointedly declining to sign it.

No one knew quite what to do. After a long-seeming several seconds, the CEO looked to his EP team for help, and they realized the situation was not normal, not part of the CEO's presentation. They sprang into action and escorted the two protesters off the stage. (It was later determined that the two were well-known environmental activists, equipped with fraudulently obtained press badges.)

Although three EP specialists were on-site and well positioned to intervene in the activists' attack vector (their route to the principal), they did not prevent the incident, thinking it was a legitimate activity. Metaphorically speaking, no bell rang, no starting pistol fired, no one pulled the rip cord—the EP specialists were ready but did not make the decision to intercept the activists or even pull them off the stage until they had successfully interrupted and embarrassed the principal.

In response to that episode, the EP program now

conducts rehearsals of such events so security staff will know what should or should not take place.

Lesson learned: positioning is important, but it must be accompanied by decisiveness.

This chapter updates and builds on earlier treatments of "working the principal" in *The Art of Executive Protection* and *Executive Protection: New Solutions for a New Era.* Specifically, this chapter examines the attack vector and applies countersurveillance to close-in protection, resulting in a different protective approach with some distinct advantages.

Attack Vector: Concept and Significance

The following diagram depicts the attack vector, which consists of the path or steps that an adversary takes in launching an attack. An adversary's attack vector normally comprises three major stages:

- Planning
- Preparation
- Execution

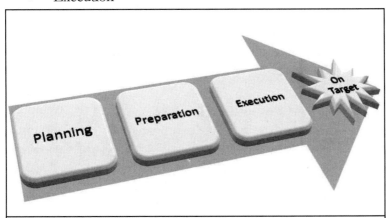

The attack vector: EP specialists want to interrupt it before the attacker reaches the end point.

The last part of the diagram is "on target," the stage at which the attack occurs. At that stage the EP specialist providing close-in protection has only two choices: go after the adversary or cover and evacuate.

A recent study of hundreds of successful and unsuccessful attacks against principals offers several useful insights that can guide EP planning, especially planning focused on interrupting the attack vector and making the decision to act. The following are a few highlights from its findings:[24]

- In the United States, attacks (in the study's database) were undertaken by lone assailants 87 percent of the time.

- Attacks in the United States were about as likely to be indoors as outdoors (53 percent versus 47 percent).

- In the United States, handguns were more than twice as likely to be used as long guns (51 percent versus 20 percent of incidents).

- Attacks in the United States were most likely to be at close range, that is, less than 25 feet (81 percent). Only 19 percent occurred at more than 25 feet. The longest range was 263 feet.

- Bombs succeeded in killing intended targets only slightly more often than they failed (57 percent of the time).

- The most dangerous place to be was in or around the protectee's car. Sixty-four percent of attacks happen when the protected person is in or around the car, and those attacks succeeded an astonishing 77 percent of the time.

---

[24] Gavin de Becker, Tom Taylor, and Jeff Marquart, *Just 2 Seconds* (Studio City, California: The Gavin de Becker Center for the Study and Reduction of Violence, 2008), pp. 7-8.

As a theoretical construct, the attack vector is not just the spatial path from attacker to principal; it also consists of the many factors and steps that may have been woven into the attack plan, including the size of the attack party, the degree of planning and research devoted to the attack, and the types of weapons selected.

Thus, an attack vector may be weaker or stronger, depending on the totality of those factors:

- **Weak**
  - — Minimal planning
  - — Single attacker
  - — Simple weaponry (guns, knives)
  - — Close proximity to principal required
- **Strong**
  - — Thorough planning (including intelligence collection)
  - — Multiple attackers
  - — Advanced weapons (explosives, rifles) and appropriate training
  - — Feasible to attack from greater distance

In words and diagrams, this chapter shows how a protective detail can position itself around a principal to detect and interrupt an attack. The recommended method is to use an outer ring of defense, based on countersurveillance, to stop an attacker quickly and as far away as possible from the principal.

Countersurveillance

This section offers a brief refresher on countersurveillance, but readers who want more on the subject may wish to consult *Executive Protection: New Solutions for a New Era*. Chapter 5 of that book is solely about countersurveillance. It addresses the what, why, and when of countersurveillance; aspects of surveillance by adversaries; countersurveillance methods; and even antisurveillance (procedures to neutralize surveillance that has been detected or is reasonably suspected).

What is countersurveillance? Adversaries who wish to attack a principal almost always conduct surveillance to learn about the principal: his or her appearance, commuting routes, travel practices, residential and office security measures, and the executive protection detail itself. Case studies prove that adversaries watch before they strike. Fortunately, adversaries' surveillance activities can be turned against them.

> **With countersurveillance, the EP specialist can watch the watchers and provide an outer ring of defense.**

An EP specialist playing a countersurveillance role maintains an undercover posture and creates an outer ring of defense. To the untrained eye, the person appears to be a normal bystander and not in any way part of the protective team. This low profile approach may seem passive, as it aims to disguise the EP specialist who is performing countersurveillance. However, in reality, if the countersurveillance agent sees a threat, he immediately takes an active role, intervening to stop the attack.

The period of watching exposes the adversary to surveillance in reverse—that is, countersurveillance, or the practice of watching the watchers. For example, at an event at which the principal will be speaking, the main EP detail may stand near the principal, but another member of the EP team may be assigned to blend into—and conduct countersurveillance on—the audience. The EP specialist conducting countersurveillance looks carefully and subtly to see whether anyone is photographing the security operation, taking notes on protective measures, touching what might be a concealed weapon, or exhibiting signs of stress that could be related to an impending attack. Some adversaries watch their targets so intently that they can be detected and their plans stopped.

The countersurveillance agent's undercover status is essential. The close-in protection team (the inner ring) should do nothing that blows their outer ring's cover or reveals their joint strategy. The ability to work in tandem and stay disconnected can be a challenge. Extensive training and practical exercises can ensure the correct positioning and coverage for the protective detail.

One recommendation the author often makes to corporate EP details is to conduct periodic plainclothes countersurveillance at public events attended by the principals. On occasion, the executive protection operation should plant some observers in the crowd or in follow cars (at an inconspicuous distance) to watch for adversaries who might be observing the principals, their protective measures, and their destinations. These would also be good occasions to practice detecting the signs of who might be carrying a concealed firearm. If the risk level warrants such caution, plainclothes countersurveillance can also be performed at all of a principal's pickup and drop-off points—again, to watch for watchers.

Countersurveillance combined with prudent EP specialist positioning will, by design, change the protective approach from reactive to proactive.

Anticipating attack modes through countersurveillance reduces the range of attack approaches that may come as a surprise. As Rudolph Giuliani, former mayor of New York City, observes regarding the power of being able to anticipate events:[25]

> The thing that bothers me the most is that the terrorists confronting us like to do the unanticipated because it is the best way to get the most out of their limited resources. Now you're playing a game in which anything that you don't anticipate is the thing that's vulnerable.

Conversely, the more an EP detail can anticipate particular types of attacks, the more it can reduce the principal's vulnerability.

An especially good place to conduct countersurveillance is at a chokepoint. Chokepoints exist everywhere:

- Security screening points
- Hotel entrances and lobbies
- Parking garage entrances and exits
- Residential entrances and exits
- Roads (toll booths, bridges, tunnels)
- Entrances to corporate headquarters

Because those locations force people to funnel through narrow spaces, an EP specialist standing nearby may (seemingly nonchalantly) observe those coming through and watch for suspicious signs (evident nervousness, suspicious bulges under garments, heavier clothes than the weather would seem to call for, etc.).

---

[25] Ron Insana, "Giuliani Goes Private—For Now," *Money*, October 2003, p. 88.

Chokepoint Attack

A recent example of the significance of paying close attention at chokepoints took place in Washington, DC, on June 10, 2009, at the U.S. Holocaust Memorial Museum:

> Investigators believe the 88-year-old [James von Brunn] with an anti-semitic past walked into the main 14th Street lobby of the museum just before 1 p.m.
>
> Witnesses say he was wearing a confederate soldier's cap and a long coat, which he may have worn to conceal what police describe as an early-1900s rifle. Seconds later, there was gunfire.
>
> Police say von Brunn pulled out the rifle as soon as he walked inside, even before passing through the magnetometer in the lobby. Six-year veteran security officer, Stephen Tyrone Johns was hit. The 39-year-old from Temple Hills, Maryland died a short time later at George Washington Hospital....
>
> Two other security guards fired back at the gunman and may have hit him in the head.

A chokepoint can force an adversary to act or otherwise reveal himself at some distance from protectees or other vulnerable targets. In the Holocaust Museum, the checkpoint, which also served as a chokepoint, was the site where the adversary declared his intentions by pulling out a firearm and beginning to shoot. That checkpoint/chokepoint also provided an opportunity for security officers to watch people who were entering and thereby create an outer ring of defense.

Source: Will Thomas, "Holocaust Museum Shooting Kills Guard," *MyFoxDc.com*, June 11, 2009. Available: http://www.myfoxdc.com/dpp/news/061009_2_shot_inside_d c_holocaust_museum [2009, June 29].

Countersurveillance is practiced in many realms of security and law enforcement. For example, the Transportation Security Administration has been training personnel to scan crowds and attempt to identify individuals who might pose a risk and therefore merit closer attention.

Combining countersurveillance with attack vector-sensitive

positioning, training, and awareness creates several useful possibilities:

- The protective team changes its strategy from defensive to offensive and flips its role from prey to predator, taking the initiative in going after adversaries instead of waiting until they are close to the principal.

- The EP team can place personnel farther from the principal and closer to the attacker (to intercept the adversary earlier). The team's offensive style moves the defense to the origin of the attack vector, not its end point.

- The team expands its situational awareness, potentially improving its response to all types of hazards, not just deliberate attacks.

Countersurveillance makes it feasible to place one or more EP specialists at a distance from the principal, ideally closer to the attacker, and then to intervene in earlier stages of the attack than if the EP personnel were all stationed within a few feet of the principal.

Countersurveillance

- Move EP personnel away from the principal and into the **origins** of the attack vector

- Offensive strategy: from prey to predator
- Expands situational awareness

Another advantage to using countersurveillance—an outer ring of protection—is that it may be a more acceptable way to protect a reluctant principal (as discussed in Chapter 5). Placing some of the detail's EP specialists in that role reduces the profile of the detail and gives the protective mission more flexibility to carry out its mission.

Intercepting the Attack Vector

If an adversary is on the scene and prepared to attack the principal, the EP team's greatest defense is distance—that is, distance between the principal and the attacker. The risk to the principal is especially great if the

Proximity plus predictability equals disaster.

attacker can find out the where he or she will be and then get close. In other words, proximity plus predictability equals disaster.

The following graphics may provide an easy way to visualize the relationships between proximity and predictability:

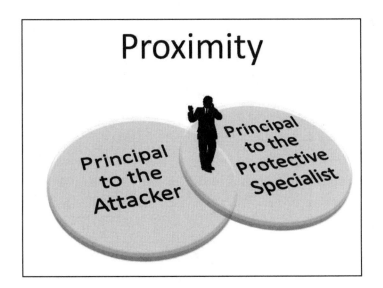

Many factors combine to make the attacker-to-principal distance a powerful defense. Knowing that an attacker is probably going to be a lone gunman, that he is most likely to use a handgun, that attacks happen at close range, and that the event will take place in three to five seconds, the EP manager should make sure to position members of the protective detail around the principal in the most effective pattern.

> **Most attacks are over in just three to five seconds.**

During the author's executive protection training programs conducted in the field, students engage in force-on-force exercises. The students and the adversary (instructor) are given .38 caliber handguns, each with six Simunition® training cartridges.[26] (The handgun is clearly identified as a Simunition gun by yellow tape, and the weapon can accept only Simunition

---

[26] Simunition (www.simunition.com) is a product line of General Dynamics Ordnance and Tactical Systems Canada Inc. It is a special ammunition designed to support realistic firearms training.

rounds.) A Simunition-trained safety officer supervises each drill.

The students are then placed into a scenario where they are responsible for the protection of their principal. As the exercise plays forward, the students are confronted by the adversary, who is gun ready. The attacker sees his chance, and in a flash he fires his weapon at the principal. The student closest to the principal is unable to draw his weapon and realizes his principal has been hit numerous times.

The distance in most of these exercises is 15-20 feet. To judge that distance in the field, the student can picture the length of a car, the width of a kitchen, or the distance from the hoop to the three-point line in basketball.

The concept in executive protection is to prevent an attacker from approaching the principal. If an attacker enters the protective team's space, the goal is keep him as far away from the principal as possible.

An attacker who manages to get close to a principal creates an attack vector with limited opportunity for response, as the graphic on the following page shows.

Basically, if the attacker can be detected at a greater distance from the principal, the EP specialist has more time to intercept the attacker in his rush toward the principal, and the attacker may have to attempt a shot (if using a firearm) from farther out, with much less accuracy.

How do these concepts (especially countersurveillance and distance) affect operational, on-the-ground EP? In a protective detail that did not employ countersurveillance, EP specialists might arrange themselves closely round a principal. That arrangement puts more protectors within arm's reach of the principal, an arrangement that has its advantages, yet the protective team can only operate defensively and cannot intercept the attacker until the attacker is well within effective range of the principal.

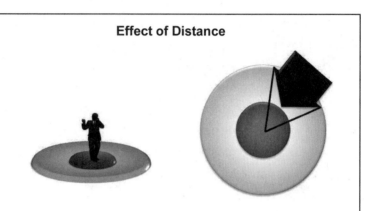

Effect of Distance

Above: Attacker in close proximity to the principal creates an attack vector with limited opportunity for response.

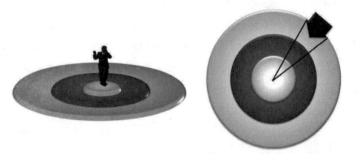

Above: Increasing the physical distance between the principal and the attacker weakens the attack vector and improves the effectiveness of EP specialists. As proximity expands, the planning and competency requirements of the attacker increase exponentially.

By contrast, as the next graphic shows, a protective approach that employs countersurveillance increases the EP team's chances of detecting an attacker (by scanning the crowd from more angles), increases its chances of intercepting the attacker farther from the principal, and hence improves its lik e-lihood of keeping the attacker from coming within effective range of the principal.

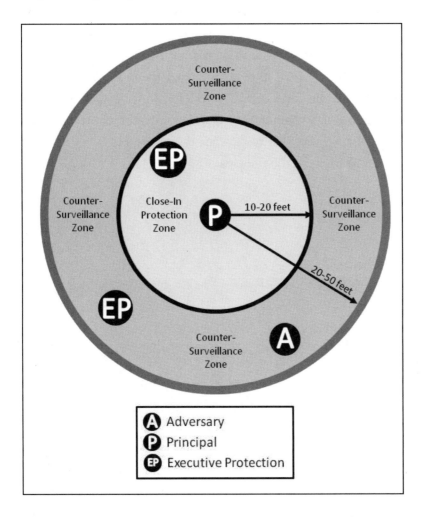

Thus, without increasing staffing or other resources, in many settings the EP team can better protect the principal by thoughtfully combining the concepts of countersurveillance and attack vector interception into a more offensive strategy.

To return to the tale from the field that began this chapter, if the EP detail protecting the executive had embedded a countersurveillance team at the event before the arrival of the principal, they would have had the opportunity to observe the crowd, see where the press area was located, look at the proper credentials, and watch for anomalies. When they saw two apparent reporters outside the press area, approaching the stage, the EP detail could have approached them and turned them away from the stage area. By properly applying countersurveillance and understanding the attack vector, the EP team would likely have been able to prevent the protesters from reaching and embarrassing the principal.

7.
Working with Foreign Security Providers

Tale from the Field

Several top executives of a major U.S. corporation needed to visit four cities in Europe. Their mission was to meet with potential investors to obtain financing support for a promising startup company. The author's firm was asked to provide close-in protection and support for the nine-day trip. The request came just two weeks before departure time.

Our coordinator for the trip would be the client's chief of staff. After many phone consultations to sort out and settle on preliminary arrangements, the author decided it was important to meet with the potential clients at their New York City headquarters.

The face-to-face meeting with the chief of staff

was enlightening. He told us about the principals, their plans, and the company's resources. The specific travelers were the chief executive officer and two vice presidents, plus the chief of staff. The executive team would be visiting London, Madrid, Rome, and Dusseldorf. Our client would contribute drivers at each location, local security support from vendors the corporation had used in the past, and general support from the corporate office in London.

Based on our risk assessment, we recommended a significant level of protective service, including close-in protection by one EP specialist, an advance at each location by a second EP specialist, and coordination of security for transportation, lodging, and meeting locations.

Having little time before the trip, we quickly made a detailed plan. The advance EP specialist would travel to each site before the main group. With a two-day lead time, he would coordinate with the local security support personnel, then head to the next city on the group's itinerary and start his advance work all over again.

The other EP specialist would travel aboard the corporate aircraft with the principals throughout the trip. Kicking off the trip, the group would depart on a Gulfstream IV from Teterboro Airport (in New Jersey) and fly nonstop to Madrid Barajas International Airport. Once in Madrid, the group would stay at a top-quality hotel with good security, and the travelers would hold their meeting at a site in central Madrid. The author would fly aboard the corporate aircraft and provide security services upon arrival in the various cities.

Without time to actually travel to the four meeting sites, the EP team conducted a detailed, long-distance pre-advance for the entire itinerary. (This is not the preferred method, nor does it alleviate the responsibility of the advance agent to conduct on-ground site surveys upon arrival.) We collected the names and phone numbers of the client company's contract drivers and other security support personnel; compiled lists of hotel reservations; noted the locations, dates, and times of scheduled meetings; and made personal telephone calls to the local security contractors the client company wanted us to use in the various cities to be visited. Those local personnel reassured us that they were professionals and urged us not to worry.

As part of the protective effort, we established a 24/7 command post in Towson, Maryland, that would remain operational for the duration of the trip. The trip began on a Sunday when our first EP specialist, Tom, started his advance. In speaking with the local security contractors in Madrid, we had requested a specific type of pickup for Tom. To see what the local security service would be like, we wanted Tom to be met at the airport by two people: the security agent who had worked for the corporation on previous trips, and the driver who would be handling transportation in Madrid. However, on his arrival Tom was met solely by the driver; the contract security agent did not show up. In very rudimentary English, the driver explained that Sergio, the security agent, had not been able to make the trip because he was tied up with other duties. Sensing Tom's concern over this failure in the local security team's very first task, the driver urged Tom to relax and see the city. He said the local security team had served the principals numerous times in the past, were very efficient in their duties, and were well-liked by the principals and their families.

Red Flag #1

Tom called back to the command post to relay what had taken place. The author contacted Sergio and in a polite but firm discussion clarified that we would be taking the lead and they should assist as we requested. With reluctance Sergio met Tom at the hotel. Demonstrating the efficiency we favor, Tom had already conducted the airport advance before leaving for the hotel. Seeing our organized, high-energy approach, Sergio may have felt threatened; whatever the case, he was unfriendly and said that, being in his country, we should do things the local, relaxed way if we wanted to be successful.

Despite Sergio's advice, Tom maintained the professional approach to EP that our firm felt would provide the best protection. Tom described the steps required for a proper advance and then led Sergio and the driver through the process of checking out driving routes, the hotel, the meeting places, selected restaurants, the location of emergency resources (police, hospital, etc.), and more. Tom shared the intelligence we had received through contacts with local police, the U.S. embassy, and open source intelligence. The local security contractors did not seem quite up to the task, but there was no time to replace them. For Sergio and the driver, the advance became a crash course in executive protection.

Red Flag #2

After a grueling day of advance work, Tom invited Sergio and the driver to dinner. There Tom had an opportunity to see another side of them. The two local contractors drank heavily and urged Tom to relax and go with the local flow. In effect, the advance process showed Tom not only the key security features and liabilities at the sites and along the routes the principals would use, but also the significant weaknesses of the local security resources.

Using support personnel to accomplish an EP mission, especially in foreign countries, requires close attention on the part of the EP manager. As this chapter will show, working with foreign security providers is often necessary, requires a delicate balancing act to be successful, and can be a particular challenge in less-familiar, less-developed countries. EP specialists who have performed their work all over the world know they cannot do everything by themselves and well appreciate the importance of finding the right security and logistical support in a host country.

The EP manager's risk assessment (Chapter 3), travel-oriented intelligence (Chapter 4), and experience should guide the decision on whether to hire local security providers to assist in the protective effort. ("Local" here specifically means based in or near the site that the principal will be visiting.)

The insights that follow are based on the author's decades of experience in working with foreign security providers to perform EP outside the United States. Without a doubt, one should expect challenges when working with foreign support; it's a complicated world.

This chapter examines the following topics:

- Reasons to use local providers
- Finding providers
- Checking credentials and capabilities
- Establishing fees
- Building relationships
- Management, supervision, and feedback
- Specific skill sets

Reasons to Use Local Providers

An EP specialist accompanying a principal through a foreign city typically aims to minimize the principal's public profile. Through the logistical support at which EP specialists excel, it is possible to move the principal around the city without attracting undue attention.

However, in a location with which the EP specialist is not extremely familiar, many pitfalls lie along the way to a low profile. Through ignorance of geography, local manners, the language, and many other issues, the EP specialist could easily make mistakes that adversely affect his ability to protect the principal and could cause embarrassment to the principal or his hosts. A wrong turn, an unintended insult, and an inability to communicate with staff at airports, hotels, meeting spaces, etc., can certainly hinder the protective effort.

> **Ignorance of geography, local manners, the language, etc., can make it hard for an EP specialist to protect the principal.**

Of course, it is impossible for any person to know the ins and outs of every city and country. Fortunately, just as the EP program may rely on specialists to conduct background checks, fly corporate aircraft, and install security systems in principals' homes, the program may also hire local resources at a principal's travel destinations.

Contracting with local EP specialists or other security or driving personnel provides an inside connection to the many factors that affect the principal's security. Local personnel may be able to offer the protective effort their knowledge of the area, familiarity with the culture, skill in the language, and understanding of relevant local legal issues. Moreover, use of local contractors is cost-effective compared to the unlikely alternative of permanently hiring EP staff knowledgeable about every place the principal may travel (unless the principal travels to only a few places, such as his secondary homes or satellite offices). Regardless, EP staff should train together so that all are on the same page.

Local security personnel, if they are of the right caliber, can aid an EP operation in the following capacities, among others:

- Airport facilitation (including assistance through customs and immigration)
- Protection of corporate aircraft
- Security drivers and appropriate vehicles
- Security help at the hotel, guesthouse, or residence
- In-person, close protection of the principal
- Countersurveillance
- General guard service
- Communications
- Medical care and evacuation
- Weapons (which the EP specialist, being a foreigner at the destination, will not be allowed to import or carry; if an armed EP specialist is needed, it is good to hire an off-duty local law enforcement officer whose full-time job is providing protection within his agency)

Finding Providers

As the story at the beginning of this chapter might suggest, finding a professional security firm with well-trained staff in a foreign city could take some work. The first name recommended might not be the best fit. How can an EP manager find the right company to provide support?

The best source is the EP manager's network: fellow alumni of EP training courses, contacts through associations (such as ASIS International, the FBI National Academy, or other organizations the reader may be familiar with), regional security officers at U.S. embassies, other EP managers known through business contacts, security staff at any facilities the employer may operate at the destination, and security staff of whomever the principal intends to meet. These colleagues may be able to recommend firms they have worked with in the past. They may be able to comment on various firms' work ethic and level of expertise.

A particularly valuable source is the EP program's own trip file, the program's written memory. This is where prior visits are documented. The file should contain critical information, including the specifics of the detail and the after-action report (which would note any improvements needed). If a security firm served the EP effort well on an earlier trip, one might want to engage it again. Conversely, repeat experiences with unsatisfactory firms may be avoided through a careful reading of archived trip reports.

There is no worldwide standard for what constitutes a professional EP specialist, and it is difficult to find a firm that exactly meets one's specifications and requirements. One possible standard to apply, at least in part, when assessing security providers is that of training. A firm's staff may be more likely to operate at a high, professional level, synchronizing their efforts and applying a common EP approach, if they are graduates of a recognized executive protection training program.

Checking Credentials and Capabilities

This task, a key step in identifying a satisfactory security contractor, lends itself well to a checklist approach. Here are some key issues to explore when investigating a security firm's credentials and capabilities. EP managers may find this research especially challenging because of the general difficulty of obtaining employment records and criminal history records from other countries. In addition, different destinations and risk levels may call for different, supplemental queries. The checklist:

- Meet with contractor representatives.
- Conduct a site visit at the company.
  — How does it feel (personnel, office, equipment)?
- Review resumes thoroughly. Verify employment, education, and training.
- Meet with the personnel who will work the assignment. Conduct interviews, asking scenario-based, "what if?" questions. A face-to-face meeting will also reveal the personnel's appearance, demeanor, and attitude.
- Take care not to release sensitive information about the EP program.
- Define the role of the contractors, specifying the tasks they are to perform.
- Find out the answers to these important questions:
  — What services can the firm provide (such as close-in support, transportation, medical assistance, evacuation, airport and aircraft security, guard service, and countersurveillance)?

- — What resources can it provide (such as on-the-ground, local intelligence)?
- — Do the firm's security employees have the necessary language skills (the local language and the principal's language)?
- — Do they possess all licenses that may be required in their field? Do they have the necessary types of insurance?
- — Are they authorized to carry firearms if required?
- — Do they possess the skills to perform executive protection work? Do they have directly or closely related experience, such as a law enforcement or private security background?
- — Will they take direction from the EP specialist assigned to lead the advance or to oversee protection once the principal is on-site?
- — Can they maintain confidentiality regarding the principal's visit and the details of the EP program?

- Discuss protocols in advance (such as the chain of command and the importance of maintaining a professional appearance and demeanor).

- Inquire about the firm's reputation, consulting with such contacts as these:
  - — Company employees working in the destination city
  - — Embassy staff
  - — Security personnel in other companies whose top executives have traveled to the principal's upcoming destination
  - — Consultants

— Hotel managers

— Local law enforcement officers

— Travel or tour agents

Establishing Fees

The author knows from experience that this can become a major issue; thus it should be settled before a contract is signed. Specifics dealing with lodging, per diem, rental vehicles, and a daily rate should be determined ahead of time. Reaching a clear understanding of the cost of using a security firm abroad can be a formidable project. Financial dealings may be among the more complicated aspects of hiring local help, such dealings being hindered or otherwise made more difficult by the parties' differences in custom, law, and currency. Though difficult, it is essential to clarify the fee structure before the trip so the EP manager can determine whether using outside support is financially wise.

After receiving a cost sheet in writing (one that notes all taxes and surcharges), the EP manager can set a budget and sort out payment methods and timetables.

Building Relationships

Building relationships with foreign service providers is paramount to the success of the EP mission. Both their perspective on operational and managerial workings and their cultural knowledge are vital. An EP manager who is diplomatic and sincere will not only gain respect but also build a long-lasting friendship and professional working relationship. Before the EP manager can effectively manage the contract work and supervise the security firm's employees, he or she should, to the extent feasible, build relationships with the security personnel who will be assisting in the principal's protection.

A major step in building such international relationships is to understand the cultures involved. First, the EP manager should take a look in the mirror and recognize the characteristics of his or her own culture. For example, if the EP manager fits some of the stereotypes of people from the United States, he or she may possibly be or come across as follows, for good and ill:

- Closed-minded
- Loud
- Rude
- Aggressive
- Obsessed with guns, violence, and work
- Overly direct
- Motivated mainly by money
- Open in sharing information
- Friendly
- Informal
- Attentive to efficiency and time management

The next step is to gain some understanding of the travel destination and its culture. Many information resources are available to help the EP manager in this regard. For example, one can find quick tips about particular cultures at the Web site of the Centre for Intercultural Learning at Foreign Affairs and International Trade Canada (www.intercultures.ca). For each of the many countries featured, the site lists details in two categories:

- Country facts
  — Overview
  — History

- — Geography
- — Culture
- — Politics
- — Economy
- — Media
- — Map
- Cultural Information
  - — Suitable conversation topics
  - — Communication styles
  - — Displays of emotion
  - — Dress, punctuality, and formality
  - — Preferred managerial qualities
  - — Hierarchy and decision making
  - — Religion, class, ethnicity, and gender
  - — Relationship building
  - — Privileges and favoritism
  - — Conflicts in the workplace
  - — Motivating local colleagues
  - — Recommended books, films, and foods
  - — In-country activities
  - — National heroes
  - — Stereotypes

Depending on an EP manager's work and personal experiences, he or she might be more or less familiar with some of the world's variations in social expectations. From country to country one may find different attitudes about many issues that could significantly affect the performance of important EP operations. Some of those key differences have to do with the following issues:

- Expressing opinions (directly or indirectly)
- Status of the boss (slightly higher than other employees or towering over other employees)
- Punctuality (expectation that people will be early, right on time, or a little late)
- Handling of problems (directly or indirectly)

Unlike the earlier task of checking credentials and capabilities, there is no simple checklist for the task of building relationships with foreign security providers. It takes the right application of interpersonal skills and good judgment. The EP manager is the customer (who, according to U.S. custom, is always right), but he or she is also a foreigner and, in a sense, a guest (who should behave respectfully).

The firm will likely have its own way of practicing executive protection or general security. Through diplomacy—including such tokens of appreciation as restaurant meals and small gifts (even caps featuring the EP specialist's company's name or logo) and gentle persuasion—the EP manager may be able to convert the firm's managers to a preferred approach.

It is important to try to keep the shared work experience positive. Finishing the task on good terms may improve the likelihood of a good experience if a repeat assignment is needed.

Management, Supervision, and Feedback

The author conducts an ongoing, annual executive protection training class in Norway. The host, Kenneth Nielsen, President of Ronin Consulting, in Larvik, Norway, invited the author to his facility to present a specialized training track. The first visit, in November 2007, provided the author with an opportunity to meet security professionals from Norway, Sweden, Finland,

Italy, and Spain. It was a learning opportunity for all—teacher and students alike.

In the training, the author discussed the challenge of performing executive protection in a foreign country, and the students, who were contract security personnel, offered their perspectives on participating in U.S.-led security operations. These security practitioners emphasized the importance of clear communication from their clients. They said they want to be told what the client requires, but they also want to be treated as equals and given the opportunity to demonstrate their professionalism. They also expressed a willingness to be told when and in what respect their performance is unsatisfactory so they can correct any problems.

Clearly, in managing and supervising a foreign security provider during travel by the principal, the EP manager should strive to be, among other things, a good listener. A venerable rhyme goes like this:

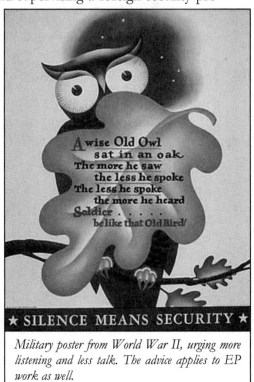

A wise old owl sat on an oak

The more he heard, the less he spoke

The less he spoke, the more he heard

Why can't we all be like that wise old bird?

Military poster from World War II, urging more listening and less talk. The advice applies to EP work as well.

Since providing the training, the author has used the Norwegian firm's support in two EP details, and the security personnel performed their driving and other protective responsibilities extremely well. The earlier training supported the success of those missions by clarifying what the author's company was looking for in EP service and creating a personal and professional relationship between the author's company and Ronin Consulting, Norway.

A good way to practice listening to the security providers who will play an important role in protecting the principal is to invite them to dinner and get them engaged in describing their local environment, customs, security concerns, etc.

Of course, as the client and the party ultimately responsible for protecting the principal, the EP specialist must also establish that he or she is in charge of the protective operation. To judge the contract staff's expertise, the EP specialist, if arriving on-site before the principal, should take on the role of the principal. When the EP specialist arrives at the airport in the destination city, the contract driver who will be transporting the principal should be there to meet the EP specialist and demonstrate his or her skills.

This advance arrival is the time for the EP specialist to offer clear critiques of contractor performance so problems can be corrected before the principal arrives. The contractors will need to understand the mission, be clear on the chain of command, be familiar with the client's standards of performance, know the expected procedures, and know the locations, times, and routes associated with the principal's planned movements. It is important to conclude each day's activities with a team meeting to discuss any concerns and make the necessary changes.

Specific Skill Sets

In some cases, the EP specialist will need to retain contractors with specific skills. For each skill needed, the EP specialist may have to do a certain amount of research to confirm that the contractor can provide the required service as needed.

Driving

Good, security-oriented driving is one of the most important services an EP specialist may have to arrange for a foreign trip. It is essential to find contractors with the right driving, language, and general EP skills. Hired drivers who are not security trained can create an EP nightmare. They may be able to give all the right answers during an interview, but after the principal arrives they go back to their normal bad habits: talking unnecessarily, driving erratically, getting lost, using tobacco products, and not being in the right place at the right time. (Typical excuse when missing: "Don't worry. I'm five minutes out.")

To improve the likelihood of receiving professional, security-oriented driving service, the EP specialist can take the following steps:

- Determine whether the contract firm has satisfactory vehicles (and access to backup vehicles) for transporting the principal. Examine the vehicles for appearance and mechanical operation.

- Meet with the drivers in advance. Determine their level of expertise in defensive driving, driver comportment (including politeness, discretion, and keeping quiet while driving), countersurveillance, and the principal's language. Ride as the principal will ride to evaluate the drivers' skills.

- Find out how well drivers know the required routes

and the necessity of remaining close to the security detail once the principal arrives.

- Ensure that drivers know how to search a vehicle for explosives or tampering and how to keep it secure.

- State the EP detail's expectations clearly before the job starts. Clarify that drivers will be required to take direction from the EP leader on-site.

Close-in Protection

This is a specialized skill, not something every operative or driver working for a foreign security contractor can be assumed to possess.[27] In addition, determining whether a person possesses the skill is difficult, especially across long distances and differing cultures. Although the EP manager might prefer to assign only in-house agents to provide close-in protection to the principal, various circumstances may arise that require the use of outside support for this inside assignment. For example, in-house EP specialists may be unavailable due to injury or illness, or some aspect of the protective assignment may necessitate having at least one local-language speaker on the detail.

Selecting contract EP specialists in another country is a task that cannot be done solely by long-distance communication (e.g., phone and e-mail). The EP manager or the EP specialist who will run the protective operation once the principal arrives must meet the personnel face-to-face, spend some time with them, and ask questions to gauge their knowledge, behavior, and approach to EP.

The EP manager wants contract EP staff who are:

---

[27] For a detailed examination of the task of close-in, personal protection of a principal, readers should see the author's book *The Art of Executive Protection* (Baltimore, Maryland: Noble House, 1997), Chapter 3, Working the Principal.

- Honest
- Discreet
- Alert
- Intelligent
- Physically fit
- Quiet
- Dignified and professional in behavior and appearance
- Effective
- Supplied with the necessary equipment
- Able to scan and calculate constantly
- Able to understand and practice the right relationship between principal and an EP specialist
- Knowledgeable about the choreography of protection (moving the principal to various places and moving in tandem with the principal)
- Quick-thinking and quick-reacting
- Able to work long hours
- Nonsmoking
- Willing to abstaining from alcohol during the detail
- Able to take direction from an EP supervisor

Once the contract, close-in protection personnel are selected, the EP manager will need to use many of the management and supervision measures described earlier in this chapter.

Firearms

Most EP work is performed without carrying firearms. Such weapons have their place in executive protection, but in most settings it is extremely difficult to use a firearm in a timely or safe manner. (*Executive Protection: New Solutions for a New Era,*

Chapter 6, It's Not About the Gun, addresses firearms limitations, permit requirements, training requirements, and travel considerations, as well as step-down weapons and the techniques of detecting armed adversaries.) In addition, the legal barriers to concealed carrying of firearms are so cumbersome and restrictive that firearms use tends to be worth the trouble only in limited, relatively high-risk situations.

If the risk assessment determines that an armed protection specialist is needed, it is advisable to contract with an off-duty police official who has a close-in protection background. The difficulties related to legal carrying of concealed firearms are much more pronounced when one wishes to carry in another country. In fact, it is hard to imagine a foreign trip on which a U.S. EP specialist would be legally permitted to bring and use a firearm.

However, if the EP manager's risk assessment suggests that armed protection is necessary to safeguard the principal on a particular foreign trip, then it makes sense to contract with armed security personnel at the destination.

It is impractical to expect to observe the contract security employees' actual shooting skills. In judging the contract staff's suitability for the protective assignment, the EP manager may have to do an especially thorough job of checking their licensing or certification, interviewing their clients, and consulting local law enforcement about their reputation. EP colleagues in other companies may also be able to share insights into the quality of the contract firm and its staff.

To return to the chapter's opening tale from the field, the author will soon return to Norway to present a third program on executive protection. The relationships developed in the two earlier programs have already paid off: since the first visit, the author's firm has already used the services of several attendees of the previous programs.

8.
Emergency Extraction of the Principal

Tale from the Field

This chapter's tale from the field is a hypothetical story based on scenarios the author has participated in with several clients. In this case, the principals are three executives from a U.S. oil and gas exploration company. The company has a cooperative agreement with Venezuela for oil and gas exploration off the coast of that country.

Unfortunately, because of increasingly hostile and aggressive behavior by Venezuelan President Hugo Chavez, the U.S. company decides to sever its ties with Venezuela. To announce the breakup of the cooperative project, the company sends three top executives—a vice president and two operational directors—to Venezuela for discussions with government officials. The company intends to have its three exploration vessels depart Venezuela soon after the announcement.

Upon arriving, the executives face immediate challenges from the blatant, aggressive street crime in Caracas. During their meeting with the Venezuelan oil minister, the Americans run into considerable resistance from the Venezuelan government regarding their planned withdrawal. They are notified that all the company's shore-based assets in Venezuela are subject to immediate seizure, including their vehicles, offices, and aircraft.

Upon departing the meeting, the executives learn that their company's three vessels have safely cleared the territorial waters of Venezuela. Their immediate objective is now to get out of the country. Deteriorating conditions in Venezuela have disrupted many airports and seaports. The safest path back to the United States appears to lead through Colombia (which shares Venezuela's western border), where a private aircraft could be contracted to evacuate the principals safely.

This chapter will use the preceding scenario to illustrate the process of preparing for and executing the extraction of traveling principals.

Role of Extraction

In a global economy, business opportunities sometimes lie in dangerous locales. In their travels, corporate executives may face out-of-control street crime, kidnapping risks, violent civil unrest, nationalization of company property, and even intimidation from governments. Extremes of nature—hurricanes, tsunamis, earthquakes—can challenge even the best-laid travel security plans. Extracting a protectee from a dangerous place requires careful planning in advance and complex maneuvers on-site. (See accompanying box.)

Extraction Tasks and Challenges

EP specialists responsible for an emergency evacuation of a principal must do the following:

- Arrange evacuation resources before the trip.
- Monitor in-country risk elements (political, security, and natural events).
- Be able to make important decisions with imperfect information.
- Employ local resources and contacts.
- Find temporary safe havens.
- Get the principal back home safely.

In the context of executive protection, emergency extraction means the prompt removal of the principal from a location where his or her security cannot be assured. Usually emergency extraction follows a sudden, unexpected event. If the event (injury, riots, coups d'état) was predictable, the principal probably should not have been in that location at that time. Also, emergency extraction is usually considered a task for a principal traveling outside his or her home country.

However, depending on the world's events, principals may just as well need to be extracted from one city in their own country to another. Fortunate were the executives whose protection details helped them evacuate New York City on September 11, 2001, and return to their businesses elsewhere. Moreover, the site where top executives spend more time than any other single place—corporate headquarters—could also suffer an emergency calling for evacuation. EP planning for such an event should, in most cases, be coordinated with overall business continuity planning. (A discussion of partnerships between the EP program and a company's business continuity function can be found in Chapter 9, Human Factor: Training and Partnerships.)

Turbulent Sites

The word *crisis* in the context of executive protection may suggest inadequate planning. EP at its best keeps crises away from the principal, either through avoidance of high-risk settings, provision of sufficient security measures to overcome the risks, or quick removal of the principal from the scene of an emergency. EP specialists use their skills, information, and resources to keep crises and their principals far apart. Still, the world is full of surprises:

> **EP specialists use their skills, information, and resources to keep crises and their principals far apart.**

- **Crime and corruption.** One of the author's clients—a major, U.S.-based multinational corporation—had no idea of the risks its executives were taking until the author asked the executives directly about any dangerous incidents they might have experienced on their trips during a risk assessment interview. They immediately recited the following stories about experiences from just the preceding six months:

  — At company sites that the executives tended to visit in Latin America, the following crimes had recently occurred: armed robbery, carjacking, kidnapping, gunfire at a bus carrying company employees, the shooting death of a local company manager, and the stabbing of a manager by an employee.

— One top executive reported that when he was visiting Brazil, the car in which he was riding was pulled over by armed men in what appeared to be a police car. The apparent attackers pointed guns at the executive's car. The security vehicle following the principal's car pulled over, and the security staff talked to the attackers and convinced them to move along. Regardless of whether the armed persons were real police, such an incident is extremely dangerous.

— A different executive of the same company said he was riding in a protected vehicle on a toll road in Mexico. At the toll booth, with the gate down, his vehicle was blocked in by a pickup truck carrying six armed men. There was much yelling and brandishing of weapons, but finally the situation calmed and his car was able to leave. He never determined exactly what had happened, but it was clearly a dangerous encounter.

— The company's chief executive officer expressed dismay over the freewheeling gun handling practiced by his local security detail on a trip to Argentina. One of the guards kept his pistol out but concealed under a sport coat draped over his arm, even while standing next to the CEO in a crowded elevator. The CEO was concerned, rightly, that accidental jostling in the elevator could have led to a discharge of the gun.

• **Terrorist attacks.** On November 26, 2008, beginning a little after 8:30 pm, 10 gunmen from Pakistan arrived in Mumbai, India, from their pirated boat. They set out toward key targets around the city. They used numerous bombs, firearms, and hand grenades to attack the Chhatrapati Shivaji (Victoria) Terminus, the city's busiest railway station; a tourist restaurant called the Leopold Cafe; the city's Jewish center (Nariman House); the Taj Mahal Palace and Oberoi hotels; a hospital; a movie theater; several taxis; and other locations. Mumbai police and security forces were not able to put a final stop to the attacks until almost two and a half days later. During the attack period, an estimated 173 people were killed and 308 wounded.[28]

Almost 20 percent of the dead were foreigners visiting from other countries, and several of those killed were prominent persons—VIPs at levels that would often call for EP service. For example:[29]

A 73-year-old Cypriot émigré who made a fortune chartering luxury yachts was named tonight as the only Briton known to have been killed in the Bombay terror attacks.

The city's St George's hospital confirmed that Andreas Liveras died last night after receiving multiple gunshot wounds at the Taj [Mahal] Palace Hotel. He had gone to the hotel for a meal.

Mr Liveras moved to Britain in 1963 and built up an estimated fortune of £315 million. He was ranked 265 in this year's Sunday Times Rich List.

---

[28] Somini Sengupt, "A Dossier Gives Details of Mumbai Attacks," *The New York Times*, January 6, 2009, p. A5. Available: http://www.nytimes.com/2009/01/07/world/asia/07india.html [2009, May 27].

[29] Philippe Naughton, "British Yachting Tycoon Andreas Liveras Killed in Bombay Terror Attacks," *Times Online*, November 27, 2008. Available: http://www.timesonline.co.uk/tol/news/world/asia/article5246974.ece [2009, May 27].

> As the attacks unfolded Mr Liveras had given an interview to the BBC from the Taj and said that he was among a big group hiding in a basement.

Many cities have experienced terrorist attacks that might necessitate a hurried, unscheduled departure by the principal.

- **Medical emergencies.** Executives who travel abroad regularly have a significant statistical likelihood of experiencing a medical emergency when they are away from home—simply by virtue of being away many days of the year. In addition, travel exertion, business stress, unfamiliar food, and challenging altitude and weather may affect a principal's health when he or she is traveling. Automobile or other accidents (even ankle sprains), as well as criminal attacks, may also occur when the principal is traveling abroad. Any of these types of incidents could lead to a need for evacuation. For minor problems, the EP specialist may primarily need to arrange for the principal to return home earlier than planned. For major medical problems, the EP specialist may need to call on a commercial medical evacuation specialty company.

- **Extremes of nature.** In case of a hurricane, flood, tsunami, earthquake, wildfire, or other major natural disaster, the principal may require an emergency evacuation. The extreme conditions may affect the airports, seaports, or roads that the principal would normally use when leaving, or it may simply be necessary to arrange an earlier departure than planned in order to flee a coming disaster, and travel hubs may be swamped by others who are trying to leave.

In the face of a severe and widespread disaster, such as the December 26, 2004, tsunami that started in the Indian Ocean, an EP specialist could face an especially challenging task in attempting to evacuate the principal from the area before or after the event. In the case of the Indian Ocean tsunami, no advance evacuation was possible because there was no advance notice of the event. After the tsunami struck, departing the scene was made difficult by the overwhelming scale of the disaster, in terms of both deaths and physical destruction. The tsunami left an estimated 170,000-250,000 people dead.[30] More than a dozen countries bordering the Indian Ocean suffered deaths in the disaster. Roads, seaports, and airports were literally swamped by the flooding and figuratively swamped by refugees.

Local residents were not the only ones to perish. Approximately 9,000 foreign tourists (mostly Europeans) were among the dead or missing. Sweden alone lost 543 citizens who were vacationing in the tsunami areas.[31]

In executive protection, one often remarks on the dangers of being in the wrong place at the wrong time (in other words, being harmed by attacks or incidents that did not specifically target the principal but that caught him or her in their net anyway). Any protectees along the vast shores of the Indian Ocean on Decem-

[30] "Southeast Asia Tsunami," United Nations Office for the Coordination of Humanitarian Affairs. Available: http://ochaonline.un.org [2009, May 24].
[31] "Sweden Aide Quits," *BBN News*, November 1, 2007. Available: http://news.bbc.co.uk/2/hi/europe/7072934.stm [2009, May 28].

ber 26, 2004, could hardly have been in a worse place at a worse time. However, at least an executive receiving proper EP service would have a better than average chance of escaping the scene because the EP specialist would have devised a multi-option evacuation plan before the trip.

Any of the preceding types of events could lead to the need to evacuate the principal from the site.

Extraction is the last step in a long chain of EP travel security planning—a step one hopes to avoid but should be ready to carry out if necessary. The sections that follow address preparations for a trip from which emergency extraction may be necessary, as well as the steps involved in putting the extraction plan into action.

Preparations

Emergency extraction should be viewed as one possible response to a situation that has gone sour despite the EP specialist's best efforts. Those efforts include numerous measures that should be taken before a principal's trip. The following are preparatory steps that an EP specialist should take before a principal's trip to minimize the need for—but still be prepared to execute—an emergency extraction:

- Liaison with emergency operations center
- Site risk assessment and pre-advance
- Analysis of potential emergency scenarios
- Security-sensitive travel planning
- Extraction planning
- Executive briefing
- Travel advance

The author's earlier books (*The Art of Executive Protection* and

Executive Protection: New Solutions for a New Era) addressed the whole process of planning for executive travel in detail. In this book, the process is reexamined with an emphasis on removing the principal from the destination quickly in case of a local emergency. For a fuller treatment of general EP-focused travel planning, readers should consult the earlier books.

This planning process applies regardless of whether an EP specialist will accompany the principal. When the risk assessment does not necessarily call for in-person protection on a trip abroad, the principal still needs to be under the EP program's umbrella of protection resources. In other words, the EP manager will need to ensure the principal's safety even if the principal is traveling without EP personnel. Through the travel preparations discussed below, the EP manager can help safeguard the principal even from a distance. Better protection is provided, of course, when the principal is accompanied by an EP specialist throughout the trip.

This advantage cannot be overemphasized. Even a reluctant principal would find it helpful for an EP specialist to be at the destination, waiting for the principal to arrive. Having a familiar face meet the aircraft provides a level of comfort and security. The EP specialist has recovered from his jet lag, has visited the sites the executive will travel to, and quietly and professionally maintains a protective umbrella so the executive can perform his duties in safety.

Liaison with Emergency Operations Center

Using various names (corporate crisis center, command center, emergency operations center), many large organizations maintain a site dedicated to collecting and disseminating security-relevant information and providing or orchestrating the response to security or other emergencies. Often the center (here called the emergency operations center, or EOC) is a secure room within corporate headquarters that is staffed 24 hours a day, seven days a week. It is the site where security staff members monitor closed-circuit television, building alarms, emergency intercoms, security hot lines, travel security information sources, local and world news, and other inputs. A well-equipped and well-staffed EOC can serve as the lifeline for an EP specialist who is out in the field protecting the principal. Especially if the EP specialist is traveling abroad with the principal, a 24-hour command center staffed by seasoned professionals is critical for support. One phone call, e-mail, or text message for assistance can give the traveling protection team real-time information and support in an emergency. The 24-hour EOC schedule is particularly vital for travelers who may be in a distant time zone.

Thus, the EP manager should partner with the EOC, which is usually run by a corporation's security department. That department will likely ensure that EOC personnel know how to monitor and respond to incidents and emergencies around the building. However, the EP manager may wish to ensure that EOC staff are conversant in the issues that arise in executive protection. For example, are they connected to the corporation's travel risk intelligence program (whether in-house or outsourced)? Do they know they should pass along any adverse information to the EP manager? Do they know how to reach an EP specialist who is traveling with the principal or how, if appropriate, to contact the principal himself or herself? Do they track threats or odd communications that they may receive and report relevant concerns to the EP manager? Do they know how to contact and pay for emergency medical, security, or transport services in other countries where the organization's executives may be traveling? Good liaison (before the trip) can smooth all these issues. When an EP specialist is on the road with the principal, there is nothing better than knowing a team back home stands ready to track down some needed information, make calls to help with logistical arrangements, or call in resources in an emergency, at any time of day. In short, the EOC is the EP specialist's 24/7 lifeline.

Site Risk Assessment and Pre-Advance

In this stage, the EP specialist attempts to determine the level of risk that the principal may face at the travel destination. Risks may be general (relevant to most people at the destination), such as street crime, official corruption, or extremes of nature, or they may be specific to the principal because of who he or she is or what he or she represents. The EP specialist will need to assess risks present in the destination city overall, as well as at the airport, hotel, meeting sites, restaurants, and other activity venues. The routes for ground travel between those sites must also be studied. Chapter 4, which addresses intelligence, describes the many approaches and information sources that an EP specialist may need to consult to ascertain the risks at the principal's travel destination.

In addition, the EP specialist may need to conduct a pre-advance, which is a fact-finding, resource-arranging trip taken before the principal is scheduled to travel. The term *advance* usually refers to the EP specialist's arrival at the travel destination shortly before the principal arrives, whereas the *pre-advance* is typically a separate trip that the EP specialist takes well ahead of the principal's visit. After the pre-advance, the EP specialist would likely return home before traveling again at the time of the principal's actual trip. In some cases, the pre-advance is conducted virtually—that is, using phone interviews, Internet research, and other methods to learn the details of the site without physically traveling there.

For U.S.-based EP operations, a useful source of travel and security information, lodging and ground transportation recommendations, current intelligence information, and possible emergency assistance is the regional security officer (RSO) attached to the local U.S. embassy or other similar facility. The RSO is a federal law enforcement special agent of the U.S. Department of State's Bureau of Diplomatic Security. The RSO serves overseas at U.S. diplomatic facilities and is responsible for advising the chief of mission on security matters, administering security programs at the diplomatic facility, and acting as the State Department's principal liaison with the host country's police and security services.

By conducting a thorough site risk assessment and making a pre-advance visit, the EP specialist can identify problems ahead of time and work to devise means of preventing, avoiding, or responding to them. A pre-advance is especially useful for an EP specialist who is planning for a possible emergency extraction of the principal from a foreign country. The pre-advance helps the EP specialist become familiar with the area to be visited and learn primary and secondary routes out of the city or toward special evacuation resources (primary and secondary airports, various seaports, highways and alternate roads out of town, and safe havens away from the city's risks).

Analysis of Potential Emergency Scenarios

In this stage of planning, the EP specialist speculates on potential emergencies that could require extraction of the principal from the site being visited. This speculation should be based on information gained in the previous stages of planning, especially the site risk assessment and the pre-advance.

The EP specialist should consider the principal's personal

risk factors (health issues, attractiveness as a target, expected exposure on the trip, etc.) and the destination's risk factors (civil unrest, history of natural disasters, susceptibility to terrorist attacks, etc.) when brainstorming about potential emergencies. The following are some questions to ask:

- Is the principal at special risk of sudden, severe illness, such as a heart attack? If the principal experienced a heart attack or similar medical emergency, is the medical care at the destination sufficient, or would an evacuation be necessary as soon as it could be done safely?

- If the principal were physically attacked and harmed, would local medical care be sufficient, or would an evacuation be needed?

- How likely is a wave of civil unrest (riots, general strikes, etc.) in the country at the time the principal will be visiting? What specific scenarios seem more likely than others?

- If a natural disaster occurred, would the site be relatively easy or relatively difficult to leave? Are the site's transportation options broad or limited?

- What governmental and legal conditions might necessitate evacuation? Would the host government be likely to support, discourage, prohibit, or ignore the principal's need to be evacuated?

- Have EP specialists in other companies had to evacuate their protectees from the destination? (Professional contacts developed through EP training and other networks may share their experiences.) What kinds of incidents led to the evacuation? Are those incidents likely to occur again?

The answers may have to consist of estimates and probabilities rather than anything definitive. However, even general answers can provide the EP specialist with direction in developing response plans.

Turmoil in Honduras

Events that could necessitate emergency evacuation of the principal continue to occur around the world. On June 28, 2009, the government of Honduras changed overnight, throwing the country into confusion:

> Soldiers stormed the presidential palace in the Honduran capital of Tegucigalpa at dawn Sunday and forced President Manuel Zelaya into exile in Costa Rica. The military-led ouster sparked a regional crisis that thrusts the impoverished banana-growing country onto the international stage and revives painful memories of coup-fueled turmoil in Latin America.
>
> The coup was condemned throughout the Americas. President Obama joined other regional leaders in calling for a peaceful return of Zelaya to office.
>
> But the Honduran National Congress defiantly announced that Zelaya was out, and its members named congressional leader Roberto Micheletti the new president on Sunday afternoon.
>
> The Honduran Supreme Court also supported the removal of Zelaya, saying that the military was acting in defense of democracy.... The coup was mostly peaceful, though tanks and soldiers occupied streets in Tegucigalpa.
>
> Zelaya was removed from office as Hondurans prepared to vote Sunday in a nonbinding referendum asking them whether they would support a constituent assembly to rewrite the constitution. Zelaya's critics said he wanted to use the referendum to open the door to reelection after his term ends in January 2010, an assertion that he denied.
>
> The referendum...was condemned by broad swaths of Honduran society as an obvious power grab. The Honduran Supreme Court called the referendum unconstitutional, and leaders of Zelaya's own party denounced the measure.
>
> The scene in Tegucigalpa on Sunday was chaotic, and it was unclear what would happen next.

Source: William Booth and Juan Forero, "Honduran Military Outs President," *The Washington Post*, June 29, 2009.

Security-Sensitive Travel Planning

The following considerations apply to security-oriented planning for any trip the principal may take, regardless of whether emergency extraction is likely to be needed. If the trip goes well, the special equipment and resources may not be needed. If it goes poorly, the equipment and other resources may come in handy. If the trip takes a disastrous turn, the equipment and resources may actually help save the principal's or EP specialist's life. The following are the main categories of security-sensitive travel planning considerations:

- **Information protection.** The EP specialist should ensure that the principal's travel plans are kept private. It may be necessary to brief the principal's executive assistant, the corporate travel department, and any contract travel agency the company uses, explaining the need to protect the principal's travel information. Leaks could provide adversaries with actionable information. In some cases, such as publicly announced speeches that principals are scheduled to give, it may be impossible to completely conceal travel plans. Nevertheless, the EP operation should work with other departments in the organization to minimize the spread of travel details, such as specific dates or flights, hotel names, driving services used, etc.

- **Safety equipment.** An EP specialist who will be traveling with the principal or meeting the principal at the destination should bring certain security and safety equipment. If the EP specialist will not accompany the principal on the trip, it is useful to supply the principal with a modest set of equipment. Usually one packs the equipment into a "go bag," a small pouch or container that can fit in the principal's or EP specialist's carry-on luggage. The contents of the go bag are generally intended to help the travelers escape a building fire or find their way to safety after a serious problem that disrupts a city. For example, the go bag might include a smoke mask, small first-aid kit, GPS device, flashlight, local currency, local map, food (such as energy bars), bottled water, prescription medications if necessary, and emergency resource contact information. A go bag can be a life saver in any type of emergency and may be especially useful in situations that call for extraction of the principal.

- **Communication equipment.** Ensuring that the principal's mobile telephone will work at the destination may be the responsibility of the principal's executive assistant, but the EP specialist should double-check that the issue has been attended to—and should obviously check that his or her own phone will work abroad, too. It is necessary to check not just that the phone's particular technology (e.g., GSM, CDMA, etc.) will work at the destination, but also that the phone is capable of operating on the frequencies used at the destination. In addition, both the EP specialist and the principal must know how to place calls—that is, whether any special codes must be used when dialing. If necessary, it is easy to rent phones that are guaranteed to work in specific countries; however, from a security standpoint, it may be better to buy such phones.

In some locations, it is advisable to use a satellite phone, which does not rely on the proximity of cell towers and will operate anywhere on land, at sea, and in the air. One can rent a satellite phone cheaply (roughly $35 per week plus $1 per minute of voice use), though again it may be better to buy one so as not to leave any details on the phone (such as numbers dialed). A satellite phone would also likely be an essential tool in the types of situations that would lead to a principal's evacuation, as local cell circuits could be overloaded in such an emergency.

- **Lodging.** Of course, the principal should stay in the safest hotels available. Typically, these would be the types of high-end hotels that the principal would stay in anyway, regardless of their safety features. The EP specialist should ensure that any hotels chosen by the principal, executive assistant, or travel staff meet the EP specialists' security expectations. Two key elements are to avoid lobby and drive-up areas and to select rooms between floors 3 and 7 in the rear of the hotel, to mitigate exposure to the all-too-common drive up or drive-in car or truck bomb. (Chapter 9, Human Factor: Training and Partnerships, details the value of establishing partnerships with travel staff.) The better hotels have advanced fire-suppression systems, fire exits that meet the latest safety codes, and typically full-time security managers, with whom the EP specialist can confer in advance.

  As the recent attack in Mumbai, India, shows, even high-end hotels are no guarantee of safety against a terrorist-grade assault. In fact, high-end hotels that primarily serve foreigners may stand out as attractive attack targets (as they did in Jakarta, Indonesia, in 2003; Taba City, Egypt, in 2004; Sharm el-Sheikh, Egypt, and Amman, Jordan, in 2005; Islamabad, Pakistan, Kabul,

Afghanistan, in 2008; etc.). As in all aspects of EP, one must balance the likelihood of an attack that specifically targets the principal against the likelihood of an attack that harms the principal incidentally (that is, because he or she was in the wrong place at the wrong time). A high-end hotel may provide good protection against fire and may have a security manager who can help with security logistics (such as quietly moving the principal into and out of the hotel, keeping the principal's name out of the guest register, and sharing knowledge of local risks). On the other hand, a high-end hotel may tend to attract generalized attacks against wealthy people or foreigners.

- **Local security service providers, including drivers.** Before sending or accompanying a principal on a trip, the EP specialist should line up local security services that can assist in protecting the principal. Again, U.S. State Department regional security officers are the best source for this kind of information. (Chapter 7, Working with Foreign Security Providers, addresses this topic in detail.)

  The level of service needed is based on the EP specialist's risk assessment. Contractors may be needed to provide guard-level service (to protect meeting sites), in-person EP (to accompany the principal to events), and secure driving service (with drivers who are knowledgeable about the area, speak the principal's language, and have been trained in the security and service aspects of professional driving). Any contractors selected should be the most reliable available and should conform, as much as possible, to U.S. security standards.

Conflicts of Interest

In cases where the principal is traveling to meet a subordinate (such as the manager of a company plant in another country), it is common to ask that employee to oversee security planning for the principal's visit. Certainly, that approach provides some benefits: the local manager is likely to be familiar with local hazards, local methods for actually getting things done (that is, unofficial solutions versus official ones), and local security resources (such as trained guards and drivers who know the area and also speak the principal's language).

However, in some cases the local manager may have a conflict of interest when planning for executive security. If security expenses for the executive's visit come from the local manager's budget, the manager might underspend in an attempt to save money for local operations. If the local manager suspects that the principal is visiting for the purpose of firing the manager or otherwise shaking things up in a way that might be against the manager's personal interests, the manager might not be a reliable source of help and may fail to make adequate security arrangements. In an even worse scenario, the local manager could be in league with kidnappers or other criminals, to whom the manager might provide the principal's travel and security plans.

In one of the author's EP risk assessment/consultation projects for a major U.S. corporation, it turned out that a top company executive had earlier traveled to a high-risk, kidnapping-rife destination to visit a corporate plant and fire its manager. The executive knew the purpose of his trip, of course, and the local manager who was to be fired suspected the trip's purpose, yet the EP specialist did not know that important background information. (Among other lessons, this example suggests that protectees should, to the extent feasible, tell their EP managers the purpose of any trips in case the purpose affects the trip's risk profile.)

Thus, when the EP specialist consulted the local manager on risk conditions and asked for his help in selecting local security personnel to supplement the principal's security and provide secure ground transportation, he was in fact working with someone who did not necessarily want the principal to arrive safely. In this case, the principal was not harmed on the trip. However, later the company received anonymous tips stating that a visiting company executive was going to be kidnapped and used to gain access to that very plant so the payroll could be stolen. Investigation concluded that the calls may have been part of an attempt to drum up business for a local security provider or possibly even local law enforcement. Either case would be evidence of a dangerous level of disorder at that destination.

Even if a local manager is fully inclined to participate diligently and in good faith with the EP effort, he or she may not have the same notions of acceptable risk as the EP specialist. Moreover, the manager's concept of acceptable security measures may differ from that of the EP specialist.

To be on the safe side, an EP specialist planning a trip should consult local contacts but not bring them completely into the EP program's confidence.

Extraction Planning

Despite any efforts to keep the principal's travel plans confidential, the EP specialist should assume that people at the destination know the principal is coming—especially if the principal is traveling to a branch of his own company. Everyone knows when the boss is coming; in-country managers may even tell employees directly so they can be prepared to show their best side. The EP specialist may labor to make the principal's arrival low-key and confidential, but among everyone from the hotel staff to the office employees to the driving service, the word is out.

An earlier preparatory step called for the EP specialist to develop a list of possible scenarios at the principal's destination that might necessitate an evacuation. The likelihood that an evacuation will be needed is, of course, low. If it were high, the principal would most likely avoid the trip altogether. However, at any given destination, some scenarios are more likely than others. Therefore, the EP specialist should identify which possible scenarios are the most likely.

Next, for each potential incident or scenario, the EP specialist should develop a list of specific, associated conditions that might follow the incident and that would make a quick departure difficult. For example, the EP specialist might determine that the prospective emergencies could erect some or all of the following hurdles:

- Roads blocked
- Main airport closed
- Secondary airport closed
- Trains overloaded
- Border crossings problematic
- Riots
- Government clampdown on foreigners

For each type of challenge identified, the EP specialist should make contact with contractors or others who could help remove the principal safely. Chapter 7, Working with Foreign Security Providers, offers detailed advice for collaborating with outside help. Because emergency evacuation of the principal is a low-likelihood event, it may not make sense to hire evacuation resources (such as locally based private aircraft and crews or armored vehicles and appropriate drivers). However, it is wise to establish contact with those resources, research their reliability, develop an understanding of the costs involved, and ensure that funds and payment methods are arranged so that the resources can be obtained immediately if needed.

It is also important to arrange for a safe location, sometimes called a safe house, in which to keep the principal if his or her hotel becomes unsafe and it is impossible to evacuate immediately. The location should have a power generator, food, first-aid equipment, etc. Depending on how long it takes to get out of the country, the principal may have to stay there for an extended period.

It is also important to identify one or more emergency departure sites, such as alternate airports or seaports or even safe rendezvous locations for departures by car. Ideally, the extraction contractor should have the capacity to send an aircraft to an open airport to pick up the principal or to send a protected vehicle to a safe rendezvous point. By knowing the location of those sites, the EP specialist can work out safe routes to reach them and can practice those routes during the travel advance.

In some cases, it makes sense to put extraction resources on retainer. If the EP specialist already has a financial relationship with the resource providers, there is a greater chance that the principal's needs may be placed at the front of the line in a widespread emergency. For example, many companies contract with medical evacuation services in advance so that when a need arises, the contracting arrangements are already in place. This particular type of emergency extraction is discussed below in the section titled "Extraction for Medical Reasons."

Executive Briefing

Executive protection is meant to empower the people it protects. The goal is not to place the executive in a constrictive cocoon but to protect the principal and facilitate his or her movements in safety so the principal can act freely and efficiently.

Empowering the principal requires, in part, giving him or her the right level of information about security concerns and measures regarding an upcoming trip. The EP specialist should not drown the principal in information. On the other hand, providing too little information disenfranchises the principal, removing his or her ability to make decisions about the trip.

> **Empowering the principal requires giving the right level of information about security concerns and measures for an upcoming trip.**

Thus, the EP specialist should brief the principal before each trip. Each working relationship between an EP specialist and a principal provides a different level of access and familiarity. In some cases, the principal may allow the EP specialist to provide a quick, in-person security briefing before each trip (at least before trips that pose an above-average risk to the principal). In other cases, the EP specialist may have to submit a succinct briefing statement that the principal can read at his or her convenience. In-person briefings are better in that they provide the principal with an immediate way to ask questions and receive answers. Such briefings also help strengthen the working relationship and may provide routine, somewhat casual opportunities for the EP specialist to ask questions of the principal. However, if a written briefing is all that is possible, the EP specialist can at least take that opportunity to spell out the necessary travel security information, including risks and security measures, to the principal.

Regardless of how the information is delivered, what should the briefing cover? In a short and usable form, the briefing should let the principal know of any general risks or principal-specific risks that may be of special concern at the destination. The briefing should clarify whether the principal will be accompanied during the flight to the destination, met at the destination, or left on his or her own. If any EP or other security staff will be involved, or if a company employee at the site will be accompanying the principal and seeing to ground transportation, the details should be spelled out. The principal should also be given clear guidance on how to summon assistance if needed. For high-risk destinations, the briefing should also mention backup plans and evacuation capabilities.

When seeking the right level of detail to convey to the principal, the EP specialist should keep in mind that it may be safer to share more detail in face-to-face conversations than in writing. Obviously, any security plans that are committed to writing must be especially well protected.

Travel Advance

The travel advance is the last stage of preparation before a principal takes a trip on which he or she will receive on-site EP assistance. Specifically, the travel advance is the EP specialist's visit to the site shortly before the principal is scheduled to arrive. Typically, on a trip with above-average risk or for any principal who routinely receives protection, the EP specialist travels to the destination one to three days before the principal. During that time, the EP specialist confirms the situation on the ground, including both risks and security measures. In some cases, one EP specialist will travel to the site in advance and another will accompany the principal on the flight. On multi-city trips, the EP specialists may play leap-frog, sending one EP specialist to the next city when the principal arrives at the first.

The travel advance obviously consumes one or more days of the EP specialist's time, but it is time well spent. Once on the ground at the site, and before being tied up in providing the principal with in-person protection, the EP specialist has the opportunity to take the following steps to improve the principal's security:

- Confirm the risk situation at the site, looking for and asking about potential hazards.

- Visit the hotel, meet with the hotel security manager, and become familiar with the building's safety features, general layout, and primary and alternate routes into and out of the hotel.

- Drive the primary and secondary routes from the airport to the hotel and from the hotel to any meeting sites.

- Become familiar with the location of any emergency resources along those routes or near the hotel or meeting locations, such as hospitals or police stations.

- Touch base with any local security contractors (guards, EP personnel, security drivers) to ensure that they are ready for the principal's visit.

The advance visit provides an opportunity for the EP specialist to ensure that all prior planning is still accurate and measures are in place, that he or she knows where to go and what to do at all relevant sites, and that security plans are adjusted to meet any last-minute changes in the city's or the principal's risk profile. If the trip has an above-average risk of re-quiring an emergency evacuation, the advance time improves the EP specialist's ability to call on emergency resources and to travel various routes through the city to reach those resources. The travel advance gives the protection detail an edge by minimizing surprises and boosting knowledge of local conditions.

> **The travel advance provides an edge by minimizing surprises and boosting knowledge of local conditions.**

Action Plan

This chapter opened with a travel scenario that ultimately calls for an emergency evacuation of three principals. To recap, a U.S. oil and gas company has decided to end its joint venture with the Venezuelan government. To announce the breakup of the project, the company sends three executives to Venezuela for discussions with government officials.

Once there, executives learn that the Venezuelan government plans to seize the company's assets. At the same time, Venezuela has begun taking military action against its neighbor, Guyana. As a consequence, many airports and seaports have been closed or otherwise restricted. The executives now need to get out of the country.

What the EP specialist needs now is an action plan. Basically, the action plan is the means of executing the various plans that the EP specialist made or confirmed during the stage of preparing for the trip. All those preparatory steps—liaison with the emergency operations center (EOC), site risk analysis and pre-advance, analysis of potential emergency scenarios, security-sensitive travel planning, extraction planning, the executive briefing, and the travel advance—pay off now that an emergency extraction is needed.

The actual steps of the action plan are as follows:

- Notify the EOC.
- Contact the prearranged evacuation resources.
- Depart.

Once the bell rings and the decision is made to evacuate the principal, the EP team on-site and back home will need to focus on the challenging realities of the situation. If an evacuation is needed, it is likely that the geographic area as a whole is experiencing a crisis. In that case, the EP team should expect fairly little help, if any, from the host country government or the home country's embassy—they may all be overwhelmed by calls for assistance. Instead of waiting for help, the EP team simply has to be decisive and begin to implement the action plan.

The action plan will need to address the following issues:

- Varying security conditions and appropriate responses
- Contact procedures
- Extraction for security reasons
- Extraction for medical reasons

The following section presents a tested approach to responding to emergencies that occur when the principal is traveling out of town or out of the country. The main emphasis is on foreign travel, where more assistance and potential evacuation tends to be needed. However, there may be cases, such as in major domestic emergencies (like 9/11), where evacuation is needed even from a city in the principal's home country.

Some recommendations within the action plan are for the EP manager or EP specialists, while other recommendations apply to staff at the emergency operations center. Travel security—and especially emergency extraction—requires teamwork by persons on-site and those back at the EOC, usually at company headquarters.

Condition and Response Levels

An evacuation action plan is typically built on a framework that matches specific groups of responses with specific levels of disorder at the destination city. In other words, the EP program should create a matrix or table that shows how to react in the face of different, increasingly disordered site conditions.

What follows is a condition/response framework, also known as an escalation protocol, that is currently in use at a major U.S. corporation. Readers may use it as a model as they create their own, customized frameworks. This model envisions five stages of conditions at a principal's travel destination and lists response options for each level. Still, any such framework, even one that is customized for a specific principal's company, should be considered a guideline rather than a strict standard. Here is the sample framework:

- **Stage 1: Normal.** In a normal condition, the safety and security environment is normal for the country. Airports and seaports are open and functioning normally. The public health situation is normal. The host civilian government is functioning normally and is in control of the country. The business environment is normal.

  Response options. Travel is not restricted, and standard security, safety, and health precautions are in effect. The EP program and corporate security continue to monitor the environment and advise travelers of occasional abnormal events or issues.

- **Stage 2: Heightened awareness.** In this stage, the site is experiencing isolated sociopolitical incidents re-quiring additional security or police presence on the streets. There are scattered incidents of peaceful public protest, and any public health situations are well within the capabilities of the host government's medical services. There is some increase in violent criminal activity, not directly affecting the principal and within the capabilities of local police to manage. The business environment is normal.

Response options. The EP team reviews safety plans with the principal. The EP program and corporate security function monitor the situation routinely and keep the principal (and any accompanying EP specialists) apprised of current and evolving conditions. The EP manager keeps other corporate leadership informed as needed.

- **Stage 3: Increased risk.** In this condition, the site experiences widespread sociopolitical unrest with sporadic violence in the streets. The instability represents a risk to the principal, his or her colleagues or family, and the company's physical assets at the destination. Intelligence indicates an increased risk of a terrorist event. The host government is weak and ineffective or is losing control, and local police have requested help from the military to maintain or restore order. Violent crime is rising to the level at which the principal could be directly affected. There may be a public health incident that challenges the host government's capabilities. There is a real potential that the overall security environment could deteriorate. Airports and seaports are operating on a less than full schedule. Business operations are negatively influenced but are functioning adequately.

Response options. Only critical business travel is advised. If the principal decides to travel (or is already traveling), the EP program and corporate security function monitor the situation closely, and the security provided to the principal should be more robust than at lower risk levels. The principal may need to minimize local movements and should, as usual, avoid public transportation. If U.S.-based, the EP program will stay in touch with the local U.S. embassy. EP specialists will begin touching base with local security providers (with whom they should already have developed a relationship) in case their support is needed (for example, for local transportation, site security, alternate routes out of the country, or other services).

- **Stage 4: High risk.** At this stage, the host country is experiencing violent protests in the streets, resulting in deaths or injuries. Other violent crime, too, has swelled, overwhelming law enforcement. Armed conflict may be imminent. The police and military are using deadly force to maintain order. Intelligence may indicate a high probability of a terrorist event. The host government has lost civilian control and is threatened with removal. Law enforcement is compromised by its own extreme corruption or other criminal activity. It may be the case that serious, widespread public health issues are leading to many deaths and overwhelming the country's medical capabilities. It may be difficult to conduct normal business operations. There is a clear potential for the security environment to deteriorate significantly and rapidly.

  Response options. The principal should be encouraged not to travel around the site—other than to leave the area altogether—until the situation stabilizes. The EP specialist should attempt to minimize the principal's local exposure, urging him or her to work within safe areas only. The EP specialist should also reinforce the principal's lodging security until the principal can safely depart the country. If normal exit routes are unavailable, it may be time to call on the company's flight operations (corporate aircraft) or outside vendors for a prompt emergency evacuation.

- **Stage 5: Extreme risk.** At this stage, the country presents a direct risk to the principal due to armed conflict, resulting in widespread death and injury. Large-scale, spectacular terrorist attacks directly threaten the population. Military forces are operating in both rural and urban areas. The host government has failed. Serious, widespread public health issues may threaten to spread outside the nation's borders. Airports and seaports are closed or under the control of hostile military forces. It is impossible to conduct normal business operations. The security environment has collapsed.

  Response options. The EP specialist should evacuate the principal from the site as soon as possible. In the meantime, the principal should shelter in place within a secure location.

Contact Procedures

On any given trip that the principal takes, an EP specialist may or may not be present to provide in-person protection. Thus, in a crisis the principal, a colleague who is along on the trip or is a contact at the destination, or the EP specialist traveling with the principal should contact the corporation's EOC. This contact creates a link through which assistance can be rendered and provides an opportunity for EOC staff to collect information that may be needed for emergency assistance or extraction. The EP manager's earlier work in developing a good liaison with the EOC may pay great dividends in a crisis. In the process of developing that relationship, the EP manager should ensure that EOC staff members understand the role they may play in supporting the EP effort.

The EOC is responsible for receiving, documenting, and managing telephone calls from the principal, colleagues on the same trip, or EP specialists. The EOC can employ many corporate assets and resources to assist travelers. One of the most important benefits that EOC staffers can provide to travelers in need is a courteous, reassuring, and confident voice. The following are some general guidelines for handling emergency calls to the EOC.

Callers involved in security emergencies may be upset, fearful, panicked, or incoherent. They may be alone or with a group, but they call the EOC because it is the only consistently available and reliable 24/7 travel security resource in the company.

Travelers who call the EOC may display various signs of stress. Reactions to the crisis that precipitated the call differ according to how the person handles stress generally, the nature and duration of the crisis, the caller's physical safety, and the anticipated extent of support from the company.

EOC staff members should understand that callers' reactions to a crisis may be immediate or delayed. The physical, emotional, and cognitive symptoms a person may experience include nausea, headache, fatigue, hyperventilation, or sleeping problems. Some people under stress experience difficulty in making decisions, recalling items from short-term memory, or concentrating. These are normal reactions to an abnormal event.

One of the first issues to address is the caller's need to feel safer (especially if the caller is the principal or a work associate rather than the EP specialist, who may have more experience in dealing with such crises). Addressing safety concerns and offering emotional support can help reduce the caller's stress level and minimize the reactions described above, enabling the caller to make better decisions on the ground.

The EOC representative answering an emergency call from a traveler in trouble should be sure to do the following:

- Remain calm.
- Speak clearly and evenly.
- Convey a sense of reassuring authority, professionalism, and support.
- Convey empathy as needed.

The audio quality of overseas calls may be poor, especially when calls are placed from cell phones. The EOC representative must focus exclusively on the caller and the crisis, ignoring other distractions. This level of focused and effective communication begins with the greeting and continues throughout.

The EOC should maintain a supply of incident questionnaire forms to help EOC staff members assess the caller's problem. The form should be designed to capture a call-back number early in the conversation in case contact is lost. Gathering relevant information from the caller and recording it accurately is important, as it helps the EP manager and others who have crisis responsibilities develop response plans.

The EOC representative who receives an emergency call from an EP specialist or the principal should take the following steps:

1. Identify the caller and his or her needs, condition, and status.
2. Complete the incident questionnaire to capture relevant information.
3. Using good judgment, skip over irrelevant questions on the questionnaire. It is important not to waste time.
4. Notify and brief his or her immediate supervisor.
5. Seek advice and support from management (especially the EP manager), who may need to engage specialized vendor or consultant support.
6. Submit an incident report, outlining the steps taken to resolve the issue and noting the caller's condition and status.

The incident questionnaire will need to be customized for every organization. The sample below provides a model that can be fine-tuned as needed:

Incident Questionnaire for Emergency Operations Center Staff

Please capture the following information:

- Caller's name, job title, and organizational department
- Caller's call-back number, including country code (or city and country the caller is calling from); collect more than one call-back number if available
- How long caller will be at that number
- Hotel (or other lodging) name, room number, phone number, and address (including city and country)
- Caller's citizenship
- Persons who are traveling with the caller
- Condition of those persons

- Description of incident or situation

Other guidance for the EOC staff member taking the call is listed below:

- Tell the caller very clearly what you are going to do. Keep the caller informed of progress, making follow-up calls as needed.
- At the end of the call, be certain to ask, "Is there anything else we can do for you?" Then encourage the caller to call again as needed to share more information.
- Test the call-back number. Tell the caller that you will call right back and that if the caller does not receive the call, he or she should call the EOC.

If the principal is in another country, EOC staff or the EP manager may opt to call the U.S. State Department's Bureau of Diplomatic Security, which staffs a 24/7 command center similar to an EOC. The bureau's emergency number is (571) 345-3146 or 1-866-217-2089.

It may also be prudent to call the regional security officer (RSO) associated with the U.S. embassy or consulate nearest to the principal, notify him or her of the situation, and solicit advice. If the call is made to an embassy or consulate after normal business hours, the phone will be answered by the Marine security guard duty officer, who can contact the appropriate embassy official in an emergency.

RSO names and phone numbers are available at the "Overseas Posts" page of the Web site of the U.S. State Department's Overseas Security Advisory Council (https://www.osac. gov/Posts/ index.cfm). When calling to speak with an RSO, the best specific greeting to get the person's attention is this: "Hi, my name is [X], and I'm calling from the emergency operations center of [company name] in [city], and we need your help."

Extraction for Security Reasons

If security conditions at the site deteriorate to the point at which it is necessary to arrange an emergency extraction of the principal, the following are key steps to activate that process. For purposes of illustration, this section examines that process as it might be applied in the scenario given at the beginning of this chapter.

In the Venezuelan scenario, the three executives are accompanied by one EP specialist. Here is a summary of how events might unfold:

- Given the hostility shown by the Venezuelan government toward the principals and their company, and observing the declining security conditions in Caracas, the EP specialist informs the principals that an emergency evacuation is necessary. The principals agree.

- The EP specialist notifies the company's emergency operations center that an evacuation is necessary and assistance will be needed. He also notifies the EP manager back at corporate headquarters.

- At present, the area around the principals' hotel appears to be safe. Because the EP specialist knows that unnecessary movements during a time of civil upheaval should be avoided, he decides to keep the principals at their current hotel until it is time to leave the country.

- Airports and seaports in and around Caracas are chaotic and unsafe to use for departure, so a departure through Colombia is chosen. EOC staffers investigate whether visas are required for the EP specialist, the principals, or the drivers to enter Colombia. If so, the staffers develop a way to obtain those visas.

- EOC staffers and the EP manager collaborate to contact security resources they have relationships with in Caracas. One security driving service is unavailable due to the crisis. However, a second firm is available. Staff members back at headquarters make payment arrangements, and the firm agrees to provide two armed drivers who speak both Spanish and English and know their way around Caracas and multiple driving routes to Barranquilla, Colombia, from which the principals will head home. (Barranquilla is the closest large city in Colombia.) The security firm will also provide a large, protected vehicle (such as an armored Chevrolet Suburban) in which to transport the principals and the EP specialist.

- Because the principals are not the only foreigners trying to escape the chaos, EOC staffers and the EP manager collaborate to arrange for two exit strategies from Barranquilla in case one falls through.

- The first strategy is to fly out on a commercial airline. The EP specialist cannot accurately project when the principals will reach Barranquilla, so headquarters staff make reservations on two different flights—one that departs a few hours after the principals are likely to arrive if all goes well on the drive, and another that departs the next morning. Even if the cost of one set of tickets ends up being wasted, that cost is a reasonable expense in an emergency. If the company owns aircraft, or if it has access to private aircraft (for example, through a fractional ownership program), the best evacuation solution may be to send a plane to the pickup point. However, this scenario assumes that no company aircraft can be sent to Barranquilla.

- The second strategy is to take a ship from Barranquilla to Aruba or Puerto Rico or some other destination that is not caught up in the Venezuelan unrest and then fly home. This is not a particularly desirable strategy, as it will result in a long trip for the principals. However, if it is not possible to fly back to the United States because of widespread crisis and overcrowding, a ship may be the only way out.

- The drivers arrive at the hotel to pick up the principals and the EP specialist. Because Barranquilla is a long drive from Caracas (a little over 500 miles), the two drivers take turns driving the vehicle.

- After arriving in Colombia, the travelers depart Barranquilla by air or by sea.

As the evacuation details are being worked out, the EP specialist stays in close touch with the EP manager and EOC staff. If the travelers will have to wait a day or two until the extraction can be executed, the EP manager can remind the EP specialist of the following tips for staying safe in a chaotic environment, and the EP specialist can share the advice with the principals and help them follow it:

- Avoid all large gatherings related to civil, political, or religious issues. Even seemingly peaceful rallies can spur violence or be met with resistance by security forces. Bystanders may be arrested or harmed by security forces using water cannons or tear gas. Security forces may be agitated and their actions and behaviors unpredictable.

- During violent or potentially violent unrest, avoid police stations (unless seeking help), government buildings (including embassies), Western fast-food restaurants, and banks. These establishments are often targeted.

- If violence erupts or is imminent, leave the area as quickly as possible.

- If it is not possible to leave the area, seek shelter in large public buildings such as hotels, hospitals, museums, or libraries.

- Avoid mosques, temples, or churches in areas of sectarian strife.

- Use cell phones to keep the EOC informed of the traveling party's whereabouts.

- Once inside a safe haven, remain inside until the crowds have dissipated and there is good reason to believe it is safe outside. Disruption on the fringes of the area may not be visible from the safe haven.

- If curfews are imposed, observe them strictly.

- Consult the local embassy or business host to stay informed and out of harm's way.

- If in a hotel adjacent to civil disorder, do not stand at the window. Keep the curtains closed and the room lights out. If it is important to observe the events outside, do so through a narrow curtain opening and stand back from the window. Turn on the bathroom light and crack the door for room light.

- If gunfire or an explosion is heard outside, do not look out a window. Stay low and get behind a solid object.

- If affected by tear gas:

— Wet a cloth (handkerchief or towel) and cover mouth and nose to assist with breathing.

— Rinse skin with water.

— Stay calm. The discomfort of tear gas is temporary, and panic may increase the irritation.

— Breathe slowly. Blow your nose, rinse your mouth, cough, and spit. Try not to swallow.

— If you wear contacts, try to remove the lenses or get someone to remove them for you, with clean, uncontaminated fingers.

Extraction for Medical Reasons

An emergency extraction of the principal may also be necessary if a principal is seriously injured or falls ill and cannot obtain appropriate medical care in the location being visited. In some countries, one may not be able to access skilled medical professionals, clean and adequately equipped medical facilities, reliable ambulances, legitimate pharmaceuticals, screened emergency blood supplies, sexual assault kits, HIV/AIDS antiviral medication, or other health resources. In some cases, adequate medical care may be available in nearby countries.

Companies whose executives travel abroad often contract with medical assistance companies geared to travelers. One such firm (International SOS, 215-942-8000) employs 300 doctors and 1,500 medical personnel and operates 24/7 call centers and medical facilities on five continents. Medical support services are offered in more than 90 languages to those living or traveling outside their home countries. The company responds to calls for advice and medical assistance from travelers, managing tasks ranging from the simplest (such as a doctor referral) to the most complex (such as an emergency evacuation by air).

The company owns and operates its own air-ambulance fleet with specialists in aero-medicine.

If the EP specialist determines that a medical evacuation is needed, he or she would call the EOC, which would then contact the medical assistance company. Alternatively, the EP specialist might call the medical assistance company directly. Such companies typically provide travelers with emergency cards that list call center numbers and the employer's membership number.

Once contact is made, the medical assistance company typically assigns the incident a case number. The EP specialist should share that number with the EOC and EP manager so they can follow up to check the status of the patient and evacuation.

The medical assistance company may help the EP specialist in several ways: by suggesting nearby doctors that may be able to help the principal, by arranging ground transportation (possibly an ambulance) to transport the principal to a satisfactory hospital, or by evacuating the principal by air, accompanied by medical staff to tend to the principal en route.

Evacuation may become especially complicated if the emergency conditions discussed here overlap. For example, it is possible that the city could be experiencing civil unrest and that the principal has a serious medical problem needing immediate attention. In that case, the measures discussed regarding extraction for security reasons and extraction for medical reasons may have to be put into action simultaneously or consecutively.

Mumbai Extraction

The Mumbai attacks in November 2008, described earlier, presented a need for evacuation of several foreign visitors, many of whom were representatives of multinational corporations (MNCs).

In an after-action report, Hill & Associates, a risk management and business intelligence firm, observed:

> The mayhem that Mumbai witnessed between 26 and 29 November marked a shift from traditional terror tactics with an attack that emphatically targeted symbols of economic strength and foreign citizens.

> As conflicting reports of shootouts at various locations in Mumbai started emerging on the evening of 26 November, H&A on ground resources were mobilized to verify the indications emerging from an intense media monitoring exercise. An immediate advisory was sent out to clients by the Risk Intelligence & Assessment function through the SMS Alert service. Subsequent Situation Updates, which included a brief assessment of the situation as well as advisories, were sent out to clients throughout the 60 hours of the operation.

The following are three incidents that called for evacuation assistance by Hill & Associates:

- One employee of an MNC was trapped on the 20th floor of the Oberoi Hotel throughout the incident. H&A was asked to help him with safe passage to the airport once Indian commandos had rescued him from the hotel.
- Police rescued one employee of an MNC reasonably soon after the assault at the Oberoi Hotel. However, he was first admitted to a hospital for a medical examination. His employer approached H&A to facilitate his evacuation from India once he was discharged from the hospital.
- When the incident commenced at Nariman Point, five employees of an MNC were staying at Taj Lands End, one of the four Mumbai properties of the Taj Group. Their employer asked H&A to speedily evacuate the employees out of India.

Source: Hill & Associates (www.hill-assoc.com), "The Hill & Associates Response: Mumbai, 26-29 November 2008," client report.

9.
Human Factor: Training and Partnerships

Executive protection makes use of technology, but the core of EP is human behavior, performance, and relationships. Optimizing those factors requires high-quality training and mutually beneficial partnerships.

Training

A downturn in the business cycle, with its corresponding corporate belt tightening, might seem like a good time to cut back on expensive security measures. However, it may make more sense in pinched times to stay the course. In a period of shrunken profits and restricted budgets, the company may face greater risks than in more prosperous times. Indeed, in a down economy, some threats rise measurably:[32]

> For security professionals, tight economic times carry something of a one-two punch—their departments typically get hit with budget restrictions, if not outright cuts, while layoffs and financial struggles tend to increase the problems security is charged with combating.

> That grim prognosis is borne out by the 2009 ASIS survey *Impacts of the Current Economic Environment on Security.* Among participating members of the ASIS Chief Security Officer Roundtable, 35 percent say they have seen an increase in crime and theft, 13 percent have seen workplace violence go up, and 9 percent have seen a rise in theft of intellectual property, to name just a few of the concerns. At the same time, 42 percent say security budgets have been cut, 31 percent have had to lay off security staff, and 66 percent now have a freeze on new hires.

> For those who head up a security department, what's the best way to navigate these rough waters? While it may seem counterintuitive, you should not feel compelled to change direction. If you've paid attention to what top security professionals have advised in these pages for the last decade or so, you are already on the right trajectory. You may have to trim the sails, but otherwise just continue to align security with business objectives, properly assess and prioritize risks, work with internal stakeholders to make sure that security is embedded in business budgets and processes, and make the most efficient use possible of personnel and technology.

One of the best ways to make the most of personnel, and possibly even save money by increasing staff efficiency, is to keep up with training. The future may see more use of training as EP programs work to provide more protection with a smaller staff and to keep abreast of the latest threats, techniques, and

---

[32] Sherry Harowitz, "Is the Downturn Cause for a Course Correction?" *Security Management,* April 2009. Available: http://www.securityman-agement.com/article/downturn-cause-course-correction-005417.

tools—and also as more organizations add EP programs to their operations.

Regardless of an EP program's budget, the last thing an EP manager should do is assign an untrained person to protect or drive the principal. Poor in-person protection behavior by ill-trained EP staff can lead to embarrassment of the principal, rejection of the EP program by the principal, or even serious security gaps that allow an attack to occur.

Security driving is one of the most important skills an EP specialist can develop. When executed well, this service satisfies the twin goals of (1) protecting the principal from physical attacks (by avoiding dangers) and (2) preserving the principal's time (by transporting him or her efficiently between locations). Because security driving plays such an important role in protection, EP specialists should make the effort to engage in both classroom and field training.

Executives receiving protection tend to be top achievers themselves, and they expect a high standard of performance and expertise from all those who surround them, including EP specialists. Several protectees interviewed by the author have described climbing out of a car sent to pick them up because the operator was a terrible driver. In cases like those, skimping on training does not pay off. And, obviously, much worse can happen than mere dissatisfaction with the driving service a principal receives.

Many organizations send staff to formal, outsourced EP training. They may send the following personnel:

- Directors of security
- Other corporate security personnel
- Current and former law enforcement officers
- Active duty and retired military personnel
- Federal, state, and local government security practitioners
- Members of private security EP details
- Independent business owners who are starting a new career in EP or building a client base

Training Content

Executive protection is a discipline with a structure and principles that can be learned and applied through training. EP training can be delivered through books like this; through educational programs (like the ASIS International two-day EP training programs or various security driving programs); through longer residential training (like the R. L. Oatman School of Executive Protection's seven-day course); and by other means, such as on-line or via video. Because EP has significant physical aspects (such as close-in personal protection, evacuation of the principal, and security driving) in addition to its more intellectual components (such as risk assessment), it is essential that persons wishing to provide EP services obtain live, in-person training in addition to any book- or Internet-based study. Live training (plus practice) is the best way to develop certain EP skills.

For employers, EP training provides another benefit: third-party evaluation of staff members' EP knowledge and skills. Typically, students who attend full-scale EP training programs receive report cards or other forms of evaluation from training staff. EP managers should request those evaluations and use them as supervisory and staff-development tools. The evaluations discuss students' strengths and weaknesses in EP issues, providing a potential framework for deployment (using EP specialists for tasks they are good at) and future training (in matters needing improvement).

EP training should do the following:

- Teach the fundamentals of executive protection's underlying philosophies and the mind-set that drives both the protection specialist and a professional protection program.

- Help the student understand what it takes to succeed in this highly specialized profession and how to prepare to enter the field.

- Discuss the characteristics of a thorough advance survey and give students a chance to participate in a table-top exercise.

- Teach students the meaning of the "choreography of protection" and convey its critical significance.

- Review residential, workplace, and transportation security elements and current, real-world issues.

- Teach both the fundamentals and the nuances of domestic and international travel security.

- Examine ground transportation security issues and bullet-resistant vehicles.

- Present countersurveillance techniques and their application to the modern executive protection method.

- Teach students how to manage and direct an executive protection detail.

The preceding list depicts the content of EP training in broad strokes. The following list names the specific topics that EP training should cover:

Principles of executive protection

Developing and using the risk assessment model

Open-source intelligence collection

Advance site preparation

Choreography of protection

Emergency and evasive vehicle operation and vehicle security

Countersurveillance techniques

First responder training—10-minute medicine

Firearms in EP (including uses and limitations) and characteristics of armed attackers

Simunition exercises to reinforce cover and evacuate procedures

Self-defense

Evacuation of the principal

Crowd control exercises

Local transport (including vehicle movements and positioning)

Out-of-town transport (including commercial and private air travel, train travel, and related logistical issues)

Legal considerations

Psychological services in executive protection

Movement of the principal in protective operations

EP specialist dress and etiquette

International EP support

Networking in EP

Step-down weapons and hand-to-hand combat

Close-in protection methods

The necessary training content changes over time in response to trends and developments in technology, law, and world events. The better training schools update their content continuously, based on the experiences of their trainers who are also EP practitioners.

Training Providers

Prospective students should consider a number of factors when selecting a provider of EP training, including practical exercises, training staff, certifications, networking, and other features.

Practical Exercises

Students should attend a school that, in addition to classroom instruction, provides practical exercises in an urban environment. The author knows the value of getting real-world experience, a chance to see how the job of executive protection is actually done.

The best EP training combines field and classroom instruction to teach students both the theory and practice of executive protection.

Good exercises actually take students out into the city to practice countersurveillance, moving the principal into and out of meeting spaces, driving, coordination of multiple EP specialists, and reaction to suspected or actual dangers. For example, in the author's training school, after classroom instruction, students are grouped into EP details and sent into the city. Instructors whom they have not met before attempt to surveil or approach their mock principal and take other steps that a genuine adversary might take. At the end of the day, the students are critiqued on their performance and asked whether they noticed the false adversaries who were trying to watch or approach their principal. The goal is to put students in realistic scenarios in busy, public settings to show them how to perform various elements of EP in a bustling, confusing environment—and to give students a chance to practice those maneuvers themselves.

Use of Simunition enhances to realism of firearms training by enabling students to use their usual weapons during exercises.

Training Staff

The school should feature instructors who are currently working in the fields they teach. They may be from federal, state, or local law enforcement, the military, or corporate security operations. They may be recognized professionals in the fields of emergency medicine, psychology, or law. The training staff should be able to claim experience, up-to-date knowledge, and effective teaching skills. In addition, trainers should be numerous enough to provide a favorable faculty-to-student ratio.

The school should also provide students with opportunities for informal interaction with the instructors. Students may have follow-up questions about the training content after a day of instruction, or they may wish to ask what it is like to work in the EP field and how the instructors entered it.

Certifications

High-quality EP training is worth the time and money a student must devote to it, but it is even better if the student can also receive external credit and some third-party validation of the quality of the course content. The author's training school, for example, is approved for continuing education credits through ASIS International, and successful graduates are eligible to receive college credit at Carroll County Community College in Maryland. Moreover, the course is approved by the Maryland Police and Correctional Training Commissions.

Networking

Part of the benefit of EP school is found in the relationships formed during the training. A small class size (fewer than 35 students) makes it easier to get to know fellow students. These relationships can pay off later when an EP specialist has a question for a colleague, needs a contractor recommendation in a fellow alum's city, is trying to find a new EP employee to hire, or is looking for a new position.

Other Features

Given the sometimes sensitive nature of the training content and the desirability of networking opportunities, it is best if the school carefully screens prospective students. The school certainly does not want to train potential adversaries, and it should not waste legitimate students' networking opportunities by allowing inappropriate participants into the program.

After the training is completed, it is also useful if the school offers students a certificate of completion, an evaluation of student performance, and a contact list of fellow alumni.

Internal Partnerships

EP operations need to cultivate good relations with other corporate departments if they are to carry out their responsibilities effectively. In the future, they may have to deepen and widen those connections, working more closely with more departments. Among the author's clients that have corporate EP programs, more and more have recently been strengthening that trend.

Why are such interdepartmental relationships important? Basically, EP is an intelligence-driven pursuit, and much of the information an EP program needs may be spread throughout an organization. That information is unlikely to come to the EP program by itself; instead, the EP program must seek the information and should also develop channels whereby the information will flow automatically to EP staff.

The most important contact the EP program can have is the principal's executive assistant. That person typically maintains the principal's daily schedule, knows the principal's upcoming activities (on- or off-site), and is aware of the addresses of the principal's secondary homes or other vacation destinations. For years, EP managers have been coordinating with executive assistants to obtain the basic data they need so they can provide protection in everyday settings and for any special events and activities.

When relations with the executive assistant are weak, serious gaps may develop in the overall EP plan. Those protection gaps are the very opportunities that adversaries may exploit. For example, several EP managers served by the author did not know the address of their principal's vacation home, largely because they did not have close a close working relationship with the executive assistants and felt uncomfortable asking for the information. Keeping an executive under an overall EP umbrella of protection requires knowing where the principal stays

When relations with the executive assistant are weak, serious gaps may develop in the overall EP plan.

when out of town, tracking crime levels at that location, maintaining a list of EP resources there (local law enforcement, contract security providers, hospitals, and evacuation routes and means), offering a professional opinion on the security of the home, and developing response plans. That protective planning can be done only if the EP manager knows the location and has built an open dialogue with the gatekeepers (executive assistants).

The principal's family, too, is a vital partner. EP managers should arrange to be introduced to the principal's spouse and identify any children or other family members who live at the principal's home. EP managers should discuss concerns about the children's safety and security at the school they attend. A meeting can be arranged with an appropriate administrator (such as the school principal). Once there is at least some relationship between the EP manager and the aforementioned individuals from the principal's sphere of family life, each side will feel more comfortable contacting the other to express concerns about the security of the executive or his or her family members.

For example, the EP manager may wish periodically to ask the executive's spouse whether any odd or threatening phone calls or letters have come to the house, or the EP manager may wish to remind the family to take certain precautions during higher-risk periods. Relationships will also enable information to travel more freely in the other direction: the spouse or school principal will know whom to call with any concerns or questions.

Many of the author's EP clients have been pleased when, in the course of a formal risk assessment, the EP manager was finally introduced to the executive's spouse and the children's school administrators. Once those relationships were established, the EP manager was able to improve the executive's security at home and the children's security at school (through the ability to make recommendations regarding physical and security procedural measures for the home and school, and through increased information supplied by the spouse and school principal). In sum, the trend toward establishing good relations between the EP manager, the family, and the school administrator leads to better overall protection for the principal and his family.

In addition to having good working relationships with the executive assistant and the principal's family, if EP programs do not already have good relationships with the following departments, they should work to develop such liaison in the future:

- Travel
- Business continuity, crisis management, and risk management
- Human resources

Other departments may be appropriate EP partners in different organizations. It is up to the EP manager to determine who possesses the information he or she needs and then reach out to that individual or department. The first stage is to meet with those colleagues and explain the role of EP and the necessity of getting certain information. Once that bridge is built, the information flow can improve. A further step is to establish systems such that organizational partners will automatically pass along the needed information, as well as any general concerns they might have about the principal's safety and emerging threats.

Travel

Many top executives travel at least as much as they stay in place. Thus, in terms of ongoing, practical significance, there may be no more important relationship in an EP program's dealings with the larger organization than its relationship with corporate travel staff. In this context, the corporate travel staff consists of everyone who researches and plans the executive's travel. Travel personnel may work in any department or position (including executive assistant), and they may be employees or contractors. (It is common for larger corporations to have contract travel personnel on-site.) Regardless of title, department, or employer, travel personnel create, possess, control, and can leak information that is vital to a professional EP effort. The EP manager should take pains to cultivate a partnership with them—for several reasons:

- **The EP program wants travel personnel to make wise choices.** Travel personnel generally book most if not all of a principal's airline flights, hotel stays, and ground transport arrangements. From an EP perspective, the ideal is for travel personnel to make choices that will support the protection mission. With guidance from the EP program, travel personnel may be able to avoid risky airlines, select safer hotels, and book local drivers that were selected by, or meet the standards of, the EP manager.

A corporate travel department may fund and even supervise the service of daily, local ground transportation (secure driving service) for the principal, whether from company employees or contractors. If the EP program has good communication with the travel department, the EP manager may be able to insist on background screening of all drivers and, for drivers who are company employees, a requirement that drivers attend security-focused driver training courses.

In the author's experience, the quality of driving service that a principal receives, locally and when traveling, plays a large role in forming the principal's impression of the EP program overall. One executive expressed concern about being driven by unknown drivers, especially when out of town. He noted that he can never be sure who will pick him up, what that person's driving record might be, and whether the person might be interested in obtaining the company's proprietary information. His unease made him doubt his safety and led him to question whether the EP was doing all it should for his security.

- **The EP program cannot make security plans without information from travel personnel.** The EP manager not only needs to know that a trip is scheduled for the principal; he also needs to know the particular trip logistics. With that information, the EP program can research the risk level at the site (in general terms and regarding matters specific to the principal), perhaps advise against taking the trip (in extreme cases), conduct long-distance travel advances (sometimes called pre-advances) to gather EP-specific information, and schedule in-person, on-site travel advances at the location when appropriate. Those essential EP measures are impossible if the EP program is not informed as early as possible about every planned trip and then given all necessary details of the trip.

- **The EP program wants travel personnel to keep plans confidential.** Depending on their training, travel personnel may be attuned to the privacy concerns surrounding travel plans. Even if they take a normal level of care with the travel plans they make, it is prudent for the EP program to discuss the particular security needs of the principal. The EP manager may be able to suggest a higher level of security for people who face increased risk, such as the principal. A relationship with the travel operation makes it easier to offer such advice—or simply to confirm that good information security measures are being used with respect to the principal's itinerary.

- **If the organization uses private aircraft, travel personnel may be the EP program's main interface with the corporate flight operations department.** That department includes the flight crews and ground crews that play pivotal roles in transporting the principal and protecting the aircraft. Close collaboration between the EP program and flight operations (often through the travel department) leads to several benefits:

— The EP manager can confirm that satisfactory security measures are being used when the aircraft is stored at the corporate hangar or at various destinations, that some level of passenger screening is taking place, that staff are following appropriate baggage screening and control procedures, and that proper medical arrangements have been made for in-flight or overseas emergencies.

— The EP manager can conduct security awareness training for corporate flight crews. Such training shows that the company is just as concerned about their security as the principal's. The training can include role-playing on how to respond to various threats, such aircraft tampering or an armed person trying for force his way onto the aircraft.

— The EP manager can more reliably count on the private aircraft to provide an advantage in evacuating the principal from an out-of-town destination in a time of crisis or after bad weather. To leave a troubled country or an area that has just dug out from several days of snow, commercial travelers can expect to face long lines and days of waiting, if they can even get out at all. By contrast, private aircraft will not have thousands of stranded travelers waiting to use them—they are dedicated to their assigned, private passengers. With good relations, the EP manager can better coordinate on-the-ground or long-distance EP measures with corporate flight operations.

How bad can communications be between an EP program

and travel personnel? Here are some real-life examples:

- At one major corporation, the principal's executive assistant, who controlled his calendar and travel schedule, refused to share that information with the EP program in any detail. On Fridays, the EP program would receive a notice from the executive assistant stating what the principal's protection needs were. However, the note might also say, "Next week, no security needed." Yet the principal might be traveling or might be scheduled to participate in potentially risky activities in the company's home location. In effect, the executive assistant was making risk assessment conclusions based on her opinions alone; she was making the determination as to whether security was needed. Therefore, the EP program could not judge the principal's risk exposure or develop security plans. It was an unsatisfactory situation, a case of being forced to fly blind.

- At another corporation, the travel department would inform the EP program of the principal's travel plans only in rough outline form. For example, travel personnel might tell the EP program that the principal would be visiting London during the next week. The EP manager would not know where he was staying, whom he planned to meet, what events he might be participating in, or how to find him if he did not report in. There would be no quick way to assist him if he needed help (such as evacuation or medical assistance). Because the EP program did not know the principal's travel details sufficiently in advance, there was no way to provide travel risk assessments or even personal security briefings.

In the eyes of some principals, safe and smooth travel may be the most important benefit of EP. This is an area in which the EP program can add value to the corporation. To do so, it must be linked closely with travel personnel.

Business Continuity, Crisis Management, and Risk Management

Business continuity, crisis management, and risk management are important endeavors in many large organizations. They may be managed by a single department or by teams of employees from several departments. Although EP managers rarely hold primary responsibility for those issues, they can gain much and perform their jobs better by participating in planning and exercises regarding those emergency-related issues.

For example, one multinational corporation the author has served placed the director of global risk management on the crisis management team. Among other things, that director manages the company's kidnap, ransom, and extortion (KRE) insurance policy and the policy's designated kidnap response organization. The EP manager also participates on the team. That multi-level linkage provides a good connection between the insurance plan and the company's response to an executive kidnapping.

In concert with other company employees with continuity, crisis, and risk management responsibilities, the EP manager has met with staff from the kidnap response organization contracted by the KRE insurance provider to conduct a kidnap response tabletop exercise. The exercise addressed kidnapping both in the United States and overseas. The response plan included a decision tree, contact lists, resource lists, and other details. It also included advice for the principals regarding security awareness, code words, and kidnapping survival. (Conveying that advice to the principals is a task for the EP manager.) In a crisis, especially a kidnap or hostage situation, there is no time to waste, and it is better to have made many important decisions and gathered key information in advance, during calmer moments.

In addition, periodically, the EP manager joins with the director of global risk management to test the emergency response phone number provided by the kidnap response group. By working together, both the EP manager and the director of global risk management can stay up-to-date with emergency procedures related to an executive kidnapping.

As they made the call together, they confirmed the process:

- The call is answered promptly and the callers are connected to a high-level response person.

- If the call is about a real kidnapping (not a test call), the responder would ask the callers to describe the situation.

- The response group might fly a staff member to company headquarters to work with the company's crisis management team. Alternatively, the kidnap response group might participate with the crisis management team by telephone.

- If the event took place outside the company's home country, the response firm would use one of its local resources already in that country to begin working on the problem until the U.S. consultant could reach the site.

By collaborating with the company's various continuity planning, crisis management, and risk management teams and individuals, an EP manager can provide and receive advice and information that may strengthen the company's EP posture. As an example of providing input into the process, the EP manager could suggest that principals not carry on their persons the kidnap response firm's emergency contact cards, as the cards might suggest to kidnappers that ransom money is readily available. (Instead, the principals could keep the number in a nondescript entry in their cell phones. In reality, it is unlikely to be the kidnapped party that makes that call anyway.) In addition, the EP manager can provide the service of

- compiling an emergency biography packet on the principal (including key facts, personal description, photo, and possibly video, fingerprints, and other identification tools),

- keeping that packet up-to-date and stored securely (in a tamper-evident, sealed envelope in a locked container), and

- being able to provide that packet to an emergency team quickly in case of a crisis involving the principal (either delivering it personally or, if out of town with the principal, having a prearranged means of retrieving it for the crisis team).

As an example of taking information from the process, the EP manager can learn about the company's many resources (such as a well-equipped situation room or overseas employees or other contacts) that may be useful in responding to an attack against a principal.

Human Resources

By partnering with the company's human resources (HR) department, an EP manager can gain information and logistical assistance that may help in several areas of EP. Examples include termination security, general workplace violence threats and trends, and thorough background investigations of EP staff or others who work closely with the principal. Such collaboration appears to be a growing, and well worthwhile, trend. Here is a snapshot of what is being done now and what can be done in the future:

- **Termination security.** HR staff tend to be aware of and provide logistical support for employee terminations. Terminations, of course, are famous flash points for workplace violence. Collaboration between the EP manager and HR personnel can lead to better security for the principal. The EP manager can make suggestions regarding security procedures, and HR personnel can inform EP staff before any high-risk terminations are performed.

  Even if the principal does not undertake acrimonious terminations himself or herself, the principal should be considered at risk of workplace violence because he or she is a primary symbol of the company. Examination of workplace shootings across the country suggests that an angry person with a grievance against the company, who storms in to take revenge, would likely include the top executive among his targets.

  Because of good working relations between their EP programs and HR departments, some companies are employing the following practices regularly to improve executive security:

  — When a headquarters employee is about to be terminated, the HR department sends the EP manager a notification that states when and where the termination will take place and notes details on any threat the employee might have made.

— The HR department has a violence assessment process for use in terminations. The department then brings in outside assistance to negotiate the exit in difficult situations. In such cases, HR personnel notify the principal's executive assistant so the assistant can help keep terminated parties from seeing or speaking to the principal.

— HR personnel are diligent about ensuring that the names of terminated employees are quickly deleted from the company access control system.

— In a multi-tenant building, company HR personnel maintain relations with the HR personnel of other tenant companies. The various HR departments collaborate to inform each other of employee terminations so all can be alert to any workplace violence that might ensue. This procedure reduces the chance of workplace violence from a terminated employee who is bent on returning for revenge. Even if the employee worked for a company other than the principal's, knowing about the potential threat, and then keeping the ex-employee off the shared premises, lessens the likelihood that the principal could be harmed in the crossfire.

- **General workplace violence.** The EP manager can work with HR personnel to institute or strengthen the following practices:

— Some companies develop convenient systems for reporting suspicions of potential or actual workplace violence. They may even contract with external firms that offer toll-free numbers to make it easy for employees to report concerns about workplace violence and sexual harassment. However, such reporting systems are not always sufficiently publicized.

— HR personnel keep the EP manager up-to-date on any suspicions they may have about impending workplace violence. At some offices, the main source of workplace violence is from domestic disputes that spill over into the workplace. HR personnel can also keep the EP program apprised of trends that could affect workplace violence, such as upcoming layoffs or news that employees have been bringing weapons into the building despite a company prohibition. One client's HR director noted that an employee at a corporate plant killed his wife, entered the plant, and was killed by a SWAT team. It was a plant that the principal had visited not long before.

- **Background investigations.** The company may already have policies in place regarding verification of job applicants' resumes. However, an EP manager who has good relations with the HR department may be able to arrange for more thorough background investigations of applicants who will work closely with the principal. EP staff, drivers, executive assistants, and the principal's household staff (including nannies) are among those who should be screened more carefully. Some employers conduct investigations every year or two to look for arrests and any significant drops in credit rating (both of which could indicate unreliability and desperation).

External Partnerships

EP managers may also find it advantageous to create or join partnerships outside the corporation. One type of collaboration that has been growing is the law enforcement–private security (LE-PS) partnership.

In an LE-PS partnership, at least one law enforcement entity (such as local police, state police, the FBI, etc.) partners with at least one private security entity (such as a corporate security department or EP program) to work together to prevent or solve crimes. The collaborative work could consist of information sharing, training, resource sharing, or even some form of joint operations.

LE-PS partnerships have been the subject of much study recently. Several research projects have examined the scope, purposes, organization, funding, and other attributes of LE-PS partnerships, both large and small. A recent research project funded by the Office of Community Oriented Policing Services, U.S. Department of Justice, is titled *Operation Partnership: Trends and Practices in Law Enforcement and Private Security Collaborations.*[33] The research discovered more than 450 LE-PS partnerships in the United States. These are some of the benefits of those partnerships:

- Crime control
- Resources to address computer and high-tech crimes
- Resources to address financial and intellectual property crimes
- Advanced technologies
- Critical incident planning and response

---

[33] Law Enforcement-Private Security Consortium (Institute for Law and Justice, Hallcrest Systems, Inc., SECTA LLC, and Ohlhausen Research, Inc.), *Operation Partnership: Trends and Practices in Law Enforcement and Private Security Collaborations* (Washington, DC: Office of Community Oriented Policing Services, U.S. Department of Justice, 2009).

- Information and intelligence
- Training opportunities
- Career opportunities

LE-PS partnerships differ in organizational structure, purpose, leadership, funding, and membership. They may be formal or informal, single-purpose or multi-purpose, led by law enforcement or led by private security, funded through dues or not at all, and open to a wide or narrow membership.

**Information Sharing Activities of
LE-PS Partnership**

- **Nassau County SPIN (Security Police Information Network).** Established in 2004, the Nassau County (New York) Police Department (NCPD) SPIN program is an email-based information sharing partnership whose members include 700 security entities. The NCPD provides SPIN with a dedicated staff of two officers and a sergeant.

- **Philadelphia Crime Prevention Council (PCPC).** In 2004, the Center City District (CCD), a downtown business improvement district (BID), and the Philadelphia Police Department each provided $25,000 to fund an alert system for the PCPC. The system has grown to include about 1,200 participants. At first the alert system used email only, but now it notifies participants via text message and cell phone, as well.

- **Minneapolis SafeZone.** This collaboration operates a secure police-private security radio system and also uses email, cell phones, pagers, and other means to share crime alerts, crime tips, photos, video, incident reports, and on-line victim impact statements. The partnership won a prestigious IACP community policing award.

Source: *Operation Partnership: Trends and Practices in Law Enforcement and Private Security Collaborations* (Washington, DC: Office of Community Oriented Policing Services, U.S. Department of Justice, 2009).

In the future, EP managers should consider joining downtown business partnerships, industry partnerships, intelligence partnerships, and other partnerships, with or without law enforcement members. LE-PS and other types of partnerships can help EP programs obtain the kinds of information that will help them anticipate problems and develop solutions in advance (such as information on upcoming protests in the company's area of the city, or news of threats issued against local business people). These partnerships—especially regional or national ones—are also useful for developing contacts and building a network that may prove beneficial when operating in other cities.

10.
The Future of Executive Protection

Several trends in the world economy, politics, crime, technology, and other spheres may change executives' risk levels and EP specialists' protective capabilities. EP specialists should accustom themselves to monitoring changes that will affect their work. By thinking "what if?" now, instead of waiting for the changes to happen, EP specialists can anticipate possible new risks and devise protection methods. The future is not yet written. By staying up-to-date on trends and tools, EP specialists may be able to better create the future they want. For good and ill, change is always coming.

In the author's training and consulting work, students and clients often ask about the future of executive protection. Chapter 2, EP Needed As Never Before, recounts recent threats, attacks, and other dangers facing prominent figures in business and government. Those hazards seem likely to continue, though whether they will rise or fall in frequency is unknown. At any rate, EP specialists generally have little power to prevent others from making threats, launching attacks, or conspiring to do so.

More predictable are the trends that EP specialists can affect through their own actions. It is in the realm of EP tools and techniques that EP specialists can actually help create the future, not merely react to it.

The following sections sketch some trends and possible future scenarios that forward-looking EP specialists may want to begin thinking about. They do not represent the whole future—just some parts of it, if certain trends continue. This chapter looks at future tools and techniques in several different areas of an EP manager's concerns:

- Tracking
- Data collection and management
- Facial recognition

Tech predictions are no safe bet, but one can be sure today's budding technologies, and those not yet imagined, will add new capabilities—and risks—to the task of EP.

Tracking

- **Global positioning system (GPS) tracking devices.** The development of accurate, portable GPS mapping devices (usable in automobiles, on foot, even on trails and bodies of water) created a very useful tool for EP specialists, who often must drive in less-familiar areas and need to be able to come up with alternate routes on the fly. Now GPS tracking devices are becoming affordable and common, providing EP specialists with a tool for tracking people and objects. Like many electronic items, GPS tracking devices continue to grow smaller and more reliable.

Some children have worn GPS watches or arm bands; in some cases parents put tracking devices in their children's cars; and persons with cognitive or other disabilities may wear such devices so they may be found more quickly if they get lost. The day of convincing protectees to wear small tracking devices, when warranted by the risk, may not be far off.

Such devices cost little more than $100, and service is less than $25 per month. How much more affordable will such technology become in the future, and how much will its capabilities grow, size shrink, and accuracy improve? And how could an adversary employ this technology against the principal? These are important questions for the EP specialist who is trying to stay ahead of the curve.

- **Cell phones.** If a protectee loses his or her cell phone, or the device is stolen, the harm that could follow is significant. EP specialists already know that personal information and corporate data could be compromised. If adversaries obtain the principal's calendar, they may use that information to support the planning of an attack. To safeguard cell phone information, many companies already password-protect device access and encrypt data.

  Cell phone data may travel encrypted across the airwaves, but a phone's identifying codes (such as its International Mobile Equipment Identity number, electronic serial number, or Mobile Equipment Identifier) may not always be protected. Already it is possible for telecommunication companies to track missing persons by triangulating the position of their phones as determined by cell towers.

Of course, cell phones containing GPS chips can already be tracked easily. EP specialists may find such a feature useful in their principals' phones as a way to help security or police find principals who have gone missing. Over time, the GPS location data could become vulnerable, handing the adversary yet another tool for finding the principal.

Security Management magazine offers several tips for minimizing the risk that adversaries could track an executive's cell phone location to deduce his or her location:[34]

— Use different phones for different purposes, "one for daily business, another for sensitive meetings, and another for traveling."

— Shuffle phones from user to user: "At some companies, certain executives will hand their phone to a colleague every week or so."

— Take out the phone's battery when feasible.

— Keep the executive's main cell phone off-site during high-risk meetings.

— On occasion, use a prepaid "burner" phone, "a term that originally came from criminals hoping to avoid being surveilled by law enforcement officers."

---

[34] John Wagley, "Can You See Me Now?" *Security Management*, May 2009, p. 56-57.

Much more could be said about EP risks related to cell phones, as well as the many benefits that cell phones bring to the EP field. The key point here, however, as with all the topics in this chapter, is not to provide an exhaustive treatment but to make EP specialists aware of possible developments in the future—and to encourage them to develop the habit of mind in which they constantly keep abreast of changes that may affect the safety of their principals.

Data Collection and Management

- **Street view Web sites.** Not long ago, mapping sites were the latest, best new tool for EP specialists, especially those planning travel for their principals in unfamiliar places. Then satellite Web sites emerged, giving EP specialists a bird's-eye view of any place a principal might care to visit, greatly facilitating risk assessment (by viewing the site's surroundings) and travel routes (by showing the locations of main roads, alternate roads, hospitals, and other resources).

  Now Web surfers can pull up street view images of many locations around the world. These street views represent what a visitor would see while driving down a street, looking left, right, front, and back. The technology is valuable for an EP specialist planning a principal's trip. By using a street view Web site, the EP specialist can perform a much more effective pre-advance (the research done before going on-site). Long before taking the principal to a hotel, restaurant, or office location, the EP specialist can check out the building's entrances, exits, and surrounding streets and alleys; become familiar with the driving routes to and from the site, including routes to emergency assistance or evacuation resources; and generally get a sense of a site's environment (nearby businesses, pedestrian activity, etc.) to facilitate movements and assess the local risk level. The degree of detail in these street views is surprising. Street views are available through Google Maps Street View. Microsoft was scheduled to roll out a rival service called GeoSynth in late 2009, and other providers may follow.

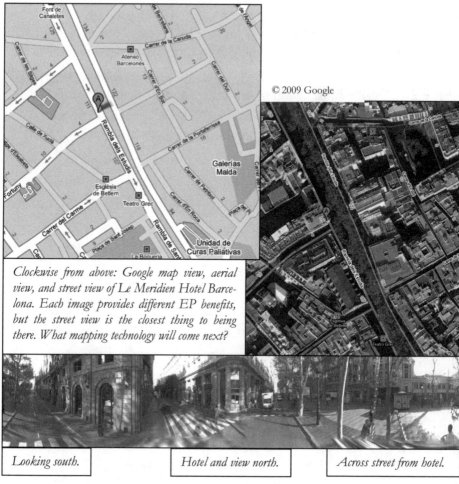

© 2009 Google

Clockwise from above: Google map view, aerial view, and street view of Le Meridien Hotel Barcelona. Each image provides different EP benefits, but the street view is the closest thing to being there. What mapping technology will come next?

| *Looking south.* | *Hotel and view north.* | *Across street from hotel.* |

In addition to making good use of street views in their work now, EP specialists should be thinking about how adversaries could use the same tool against them and what the next mapping development might be. The sole surviving gunman from the November 2009 Mumbai terrorist attacks said he and his fellow attackers had used Google Earth to familiarize themselves with the locations of buildings targeted.[35] EP specialists should be at least as well informed as any adversaries.

- **Advanced data analysis.** At some point, both EP specialists and their adversaries will gain access to extremely sophisticated data analysis capabilities. As *Security Management* notes:[36]

  Researchers at Rice University in Houston, Texas, have developed a way to quickly deduce which terrorist group may be responsible for an attack.... Ruths [the system developer] adapted spam filter technology to allow him to search a massive terrorism database to identify group attack patterns. A user plugs in details of an attack, and the tool names the groups with matching attack signatures.... [Daniel Mabrey, head of the Institute for the Study of Violent Groups, notes that the tool] does a level of analysis on this rich source of data "that is too much for a single analyst to really think about critically."

Once this tool or others like it become available, will EP specialists be able to input data about potential

---

[35] Damien McElroy, "Mumbai Attacks: Terrorists Took Cocaine to Stay Awake During Assault," *The Daily Telegraph*, December 3, 2008. Available: http://www.telegraph.co.uk/news/worldnews/asia/india/3540964/Mumbai-attacks-Terrorists-took-cocaine-to-stay-awake-during-assault.html (2009, May 27].

[36] Laura Spadanuta, "Tying Terror Groups to Attacks," *Security Management*, May 2009, pp. 20-22.

adversaries to learn about their attack methods? Or use the system to learn who their potential adversaries might be? Or will adversaries use such systems to research attractive targets and predict their movements? If knowledge is power, then superior analysis of knowledge may provide superior power.

- **Convenient data collecting systems.** New systems for capturing and organizing simple data continually become available. Given the great number of details that an EP specialist must compile, sort, and be able to retrieve, tools to juggle information can be a big help. A vast amount of data is needed for even a single out-of-town trip by the principal (such as details on air travel, alternative air travel, airport transfers, daily local transport, emergency resources, lodging and meeting venues, legal issues, etc.). One modest new tool for organizing bits of information is Evernote (www.evernote.com). A system consisting of software and storage, Evernote enables a user to put information into a searchable, sortable personal collection via many devices and in many forms. For example, using a computer or a smart phone, the user can create notes by taking a photo (and Evernote will recognize the text in the image, making it searchable); pasting a Web page, screenshot, or other bit of the Internet; dragging and dropping content into the desktop client; e-mailing notes; scanning receipts, recipes, tags, brochures, etc., into Evernote; recording audio and retrieving it from anywhere; and sending Twitter messages. That information is then synchronized across the user's various data devices and is readily searchable.

Potentially, EP specialists will be able to use such systems, and ones not yet developed, to maximize their capture and use of information. That capability will enable them to capture novel types of information quickly and wring the most value out of it. Of course, adversaries will likely have access to all the same technology and may turn it to their advantage.

- **Identification data.** Several studies have found that, for most people in the United States, it is possible to identify a person using only a few facts about that person and consulting public databases. Specifically, if a curious party knows a person's ZIP code, sex, and full date of birth, the information seeker can determine the person's identity in 63 percent[37] (2000 study) to 87 percent[38] (2006 study) of cases. (Different studies have reached slightly different conclusions.) Even with less-specific geographic data—using a person's city, town, or municipality instead of ZIP code—plus sex and date of birth, it is possible to identify the subject in 53 percent of cases.[39]

As the 2000 study observes, "Clearly, data released containing such information about these individuals should not be considered anonymous. Yet, health and other person-specific data are publicly available in this form." The 2006 study was meant to be "a useful reference for privacy researchers who need simple estimates

---

[37] Phillippe Golle, "Revisiting the Uniqueness of Simple Demographics in the US Population," Workshop on Privacy in Electronic Society 2006, Alexandria, VA, 2006.

[38] Latanya Sweeney, *Uniqueness of Simple Demographics in the U.S. Population,* Pittsburgh, PA: Carnegie Mellon University, Laboratory for International Data Privacy, 2000.

[39] Sweeney.

of the comparative threat of disclosing various demographic data." Over time, EP specialists will want to pay attention to the increasing risk that adversaries can learn personal information about a principal using very little personal data as a starting point. For example, medical or financial data that is published on-line in so-called aggregate form (without names) may still be attributable to a particular individual if the data set also includes ZIP codes, sex, and birth dates. As principals divulge more of their personal information—even on an anonymous basis—to medical professionals, government agencies, and researchers, data search techniques will increasingly make it possible to link individual principals to specific data. EP specialists will have to take greater pains in the future to safeguard their protectees' privacy.

Facial Recognition

Technology for identifying people based on their images on video continues to improve. Formerly associated solely with government use, such as at airports, at border crossings, and in high-crime areas, facial recognition technology is beginning to become affordable for the private sector and is being rolled out in new applications around the world.

For example, a British news report notes:[40]

> Facial recognition technology has long been a holy grail for security agencies, and a bogeyman for privacy lovers and libertarians…. Zycomm…offer a facial-recognition system for use with security cameras, aimed at customers such as shopping centres.

---

[40] Lewis Page, "Facial-recognition tech now used to greet hotel guests," *The Register*, February 13, 2009. Available: http://www.theregister. co.uk/2009/02/13/face_ware_hotel_guests [2009, February 13].

"This stuff used to be strictly government-agency busi-ness," [said] Zycomm engineer Steve Ball.... "But now you can get a useful system like this in the £20,000 brack-et—it's within the reach of commercial customers."

Zycomm's setup can zero in on faces from any camera, but Ball said that like most face-spotter software it only starts to show useful levels of performance where people need to move through a chokepoint facing the camera.... "Doors are OK," says Ball. "Escalators are good—we all look up when we're on an escalator."

The biz-grade spotter has an 80 or 90 per cent chance of recognising someone in its files in such circumstances, ac-cording to Ball, provided the file image is a good one. Zy-comm's special trick is that the system can then send a text message to a portable radio, saying who it thinks it has identified, where, and with what level of confidence.

Typically this might be used to notify patrolling security guards that a known shoplifter had entered their complex. In this case the file images would be those of convicted crims routinely circulated by police....

[F]ew commercial security teams can afford enough staff to individually monitor every camera.... So an educated guess by the automatic face-spotter is better than nothing.

Over time, EP programs may be able to use facial recognition systems to detect the presence of known adversaries who visit the outside of the principal's office building or home to conduct surveillance or intercept the principal; perhaps to identify un-known persons; and for other applications not yet conceived.

Afterword

Current trends in business, the economy, world affairs, crime, and technology may give some inkling as to what lies ahead, but of course no one can be sure what the future holds. Fortunately, an EP program staffed with diligent, well-trained EP specialists can use appropriate tools, resources, and techniques to anticipate many future challenges. Such a program can also develop and practice plans for avoiding dangers that could affect their protectees and for reacting quickly and intelligently to any attacks or other hazards that take place.

No machine, no computer, no technology will ever take the place of the trained executive protection specialist. The job requires human presence, interaction, and insight. The task is stimulating, and the conditions are constantly changing.

In the author's decades of providing this service, EP has always been rewarding, and it continues to be. Not only is the work an important, exciting challenge, but the field is filled with dedicated, energetic people with a thirst for knowledge.

In executive protection, success means saving lives. That is why this book is dedicated to those committed individuals who see the challenge of EP and take it to the next level.

Appendix:
Event/Protection Matrix

EP managers try to match their security measures to the principal's particular, current risk level. Over time, they adjust those measures to meet changes in the risk level. In other words, if the risk level drops, the EP program might cut back on some security practices; if the risk level rises, a higher degree of protection may need to be provided. Ongoing fine-tuning of an EP program is appropriate and normal.

However, what if the risk level changes suddenly? Changing factors that could alter security requirements might include the release of quarterly earnings statements, publicity surrounding executive compensation, or credible threats made by activists. Will the EP program be ready to respond immediately, or will staff need time to devise a new protection plan? If the risk level declines, there is no great harm in taking one's time to trim some of the protection measures being provided to the principal. By contrast, if the risk level suddenly spikes up, there is no time to ponder over which increased security measures might make sense, search around for needed resources, and consider how to implement a higher degree of protection. The EP program has to respond quickly.

To facilitate quick decision making in the face of changing risk levels, an EP manager can develop a matrix or other guideline that states which security measures should be used for various activities at different risk levels. For example, when a principal plans to travel to a corporate facility in a low-risk U.S. city, he or she may need only a properly vetted driver at the other end. When a principal plans to travel to a higher-risk city in another country, extensive extra security measures (including in-person protection) may be needed. Similarly, different protective measures may be needed depending on a principal's activities—perhaps more for widely attended speaking engagements announced in advance and not as many for private meetings with other company executives. The level of protection required also varies with changing risk levels overall.

Matching protection measures to particular activities is not a mathematically precise process. Some companies rely on a general sense of what may be needed based on the risk information they collect and their EP specialist's gut feeling developed through experience. Others use a matrix that takes into account the type of activity anticipated (speech, private meeting, termination proceeding, labor negotiation) and the general level of risk directed at the principal.

The matrix presented here is based on models used in other U.S. corporations, so it provides a benchmark. However, it will have to be tailored to each organization's culture, the particular activities the principals engage in, and the particular risks they face. Moreover, the options it presents must be considered guidelines that should be overridden when the EP specialist's informed judgment calls for different protective measures. This matrix should serve only as an example awaiting customization.

The matrix can also be designed with more risk levels to match any system the EP program uses, such as negligible-low-moderate-high-critical or the Homeland Security Advisory System's low-guarded-elevated-high-critical continuum.

The matrix approach set fairly objective criteria for which of the principals' events and activities would warrant driving service, on-site travel advances, or in-person protection (during travel or special events). Basing the protection measures provided on clearly identifiable criteria may make it more palatable for protectees to accept protection. Of course, decisions on coverage can still be adjusted on a case-by-case basis, but a matrix takes initial decision making out of the subjective realm and moves it closer to objectivity.

Overall, creating an event/protection matrix can help an EP program in two main ways:

- The matrix helps the EP manager quickly modify the EP approach in response to sudden changes in the principal's risk level.

- The relative objectivity of the matrix may make reluctant principals more willing to accept increased security measures when needed.

A customizable version of this event/protection matrix is available for download at www.rloatman.com/book.

The model that follow shows sample protection measure options for a moderate risk level only. Options for low and high risk levels should be completed by the EP manager, based on the principal's needs and company's resources.

Principal's Assessed Risk Level: Low	
Issues and Activities	**Protection Measure Options**
Domestic travel with low risk level (low-risk city and low-risk activities)	• [to be completed and expanded by EP manager]
Domestic travel with high risk level (high-risk city *or* high-risk activities)	
Travel to foreign city with low risk level	
Travel to foreign city with high risk level	
Ground transport in home city	
Office security	
Home security	
Special event with low risk level	
Special event with high risk level	

Principal's Assessed Risk Level: Moderate	
Issues and Activities	**Protection Measure Options**
Domestic travel with low risk level (low-risk city *and* low-risk activities)	• Confirm destination risk level with iJET or other source • Confirm principal's activities planned (crowd exposure, protesters, etc.) • Confirm ground transportation plans (e.g., vetted car service) • Confer with site contacts to see whether any particular security assistance may be needed
Domestic travel with high risk level (high-risk city *or* high-risk activities)	• Confirm destination risk level with iJET or other source • Confirm principal's activities planned (crowd exposure, protesters, etc.) • Confer with site contacts to see whether any particular security assistance may be needed or can be provided • Check in with site resources (e.g., law enforcement contacts, contract EP specialists) • Conduct in-person advance at meeting place and hotel • Be in place to meet principal on his arrival; escort him to hotel or meetings • Arrange for security-trained driver • Accompany principal as appropriate
Travel to foreign city with low risk level	• Confirm destination risk level with iJET or other source • Confirm principal's activities planned (crowd exposure, labor negotiations, etc.) • Confer with site contacts to see whether any particular security assistance may be needed or can be provided

	• Check in with local resources (e.g., law enforcement contacts, contract EP specialists); ensure that they can assist if a problem arises • Confirm ground transportation plans (e.g., vetted car service) • Ensure that principal can readily call EP specialist for assistance (i.e., check phone dialing requirements and proper functioning of principal's mobile phone at the destination as not all phone technologies work in all places) • Be in place to meet principal on his arrival; escort him to hotel or meetings
Travel to foreign city with high risk level	• Confirm destination risk level with iJET or other source • Confirm principal's activities planned (crowd exposure, labor negotiations, etc.) • Confer with site contacts to see whether any particular security assistance may be needed or can be provided • Check in with site resources (e.g., law enforcement contacts) • Contract with a local EP specialist who knows the language, culture, laws, etc. • Conduct in-person advance at meeting place and hotel • Be in place to meet principal on his arrival; escort him to hotel or meetings and in transit • Arrange for security-trained driver • Accompany principal as appropriate • Ensure that principal can readily call EP specialist for assistance (i.e., check phone dialing requirements

	and proper functioning of principal's mobile phone at the destination as not all phone technologies work in all places) • Develop extraction plan and medical response or evacuation plan
Ground transport in home city	• Use company drivers • If drivers unavailable, use EP specialist instead of a car service
Office security	• Establish a schedule for checking panic buttons, condition of safe rooms, etc. • Regularly ask executive assistants, visitor desk staff, and security officers about trends in unwanted visitors to building or principal's office area
Home security	• Arrange for annual maintenance and testing of home alarm system • Periodically ask principal and spouse whether they have any home security concerns
Special event with low risk level	• Conduct a long-distance advance of the site, calling key parties (site security managers, etc.) to learn about risks and security measures
Special event with high risk level	• Conduct an in-person advance of the site • Be present to meet the principal, escort him inside, and stay nearby to monitor conditions and provide assistance

Principal's Assessed Risk Level: High	
Issues and Activities	**Protection Measure Options**
Domestic travel with low risk level (low-risk city *and* low-risk activities)	• [to be completed and expanded by EP manager]
Domestic travel with high risk level (high-risk city *or* high-risk activities)	
Travel to foreign city with low risk level	
Travel to foreign city with high risk level	
Ground transport in home city	
Office security	
Home security	
Special event with low risk level	
Special event with high risk level	

Index